SHIFTING STATS
SHAKING THE CHURCH:
40 CANADIAN CHURCHES RESPOND

PATRICIA PADDEY AND **KAREN STILLER**
FOREWORD AND POSTSCRIPT BY REV. DR. DON MOORE

ISBN 978-0-921485-38-4

© 2015 by World Vision Canada

Published by World Vision Canada, National Church Engagement

1 World Drive, Mississauga, ON L5T 2Y4

www.churches.worldvision.ca

All rights reserved. No part of this publication may be reproduced, stored in a retrieval system, or transmitted in any form or by any means – for example, electronic, photocopy or recording – without the prior written permission of the publisher. The only exception is brief quotations in printed reviews.

Unless otherwise indicated, Scripture quotations are from New Revised Standard Version Bible, copyright ©1989 National Council of the Churches of Christ in the United States of America. Used by permission.
All rights reserved.

Cataloguing data available from Library and Archives Canada

Printed in Canada.

DEDICATION

For my parents, Virginia and Richard Darley, who first taught me about God and took me to church. For my husband Doug: because your love for and belief in me gives me the courage to believe in myself and makes my writing possible.

For my children: Stephanie, Mark and Jenna, because I long for you to know the beauty and solace in the Church that I have found. And for Maxine Hancock: with deepest gratitude.

— PATRICIA PADDEY

To my parents Russ and Marian Durling who, – even though they forgot me there one Sunday, taught me that going to church was an important thing to do. To Brent, my love, who teaches me to love the Church, even when it's hard.

To Erik, Holly and Thomas, our three kids who have been raised in the Church's embrace and loved in a special way as minister's kids—even when our pew was consistently the loudest, most chaotic and messiest seat in the house.

— KAREN STILLER

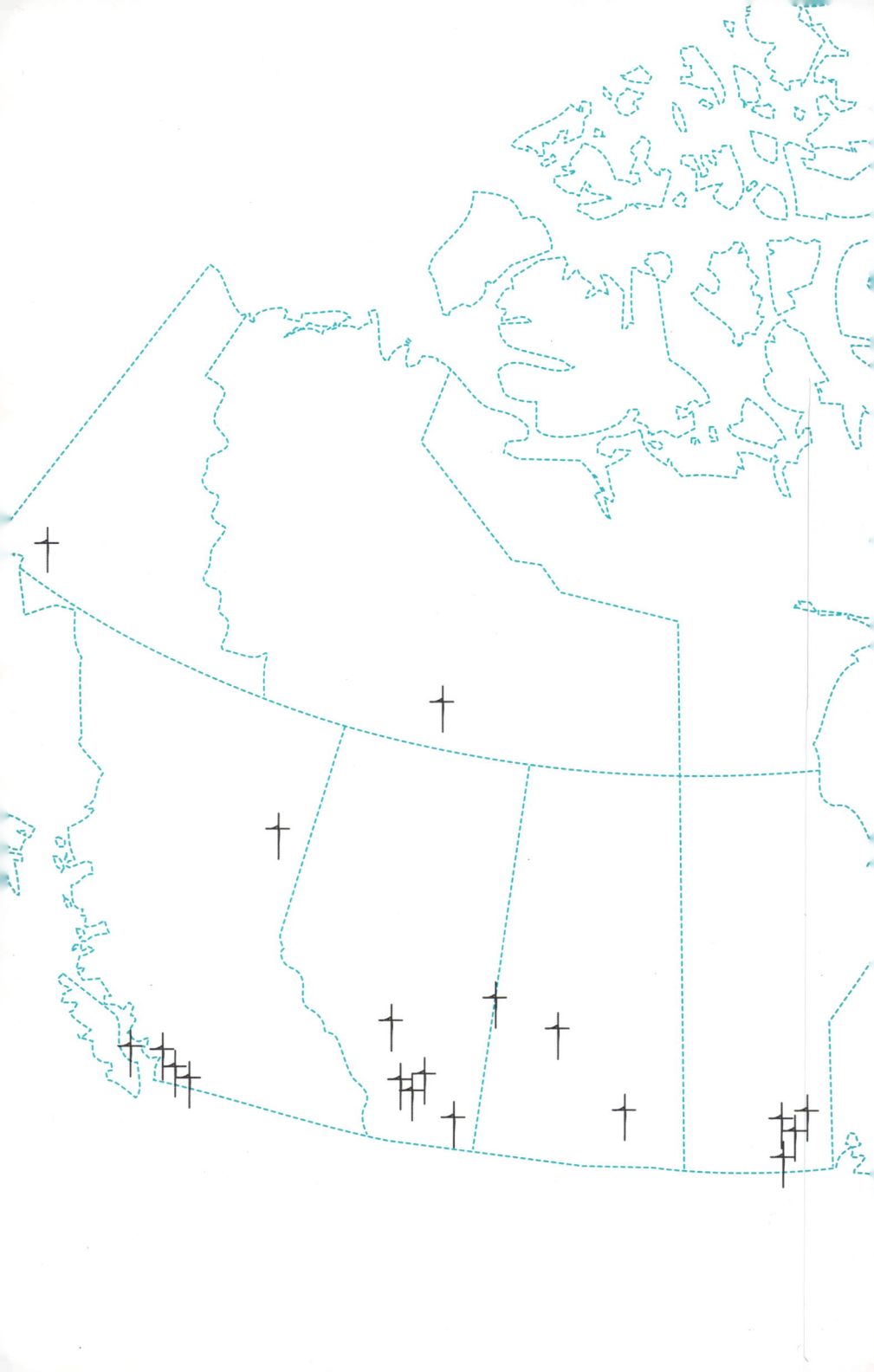

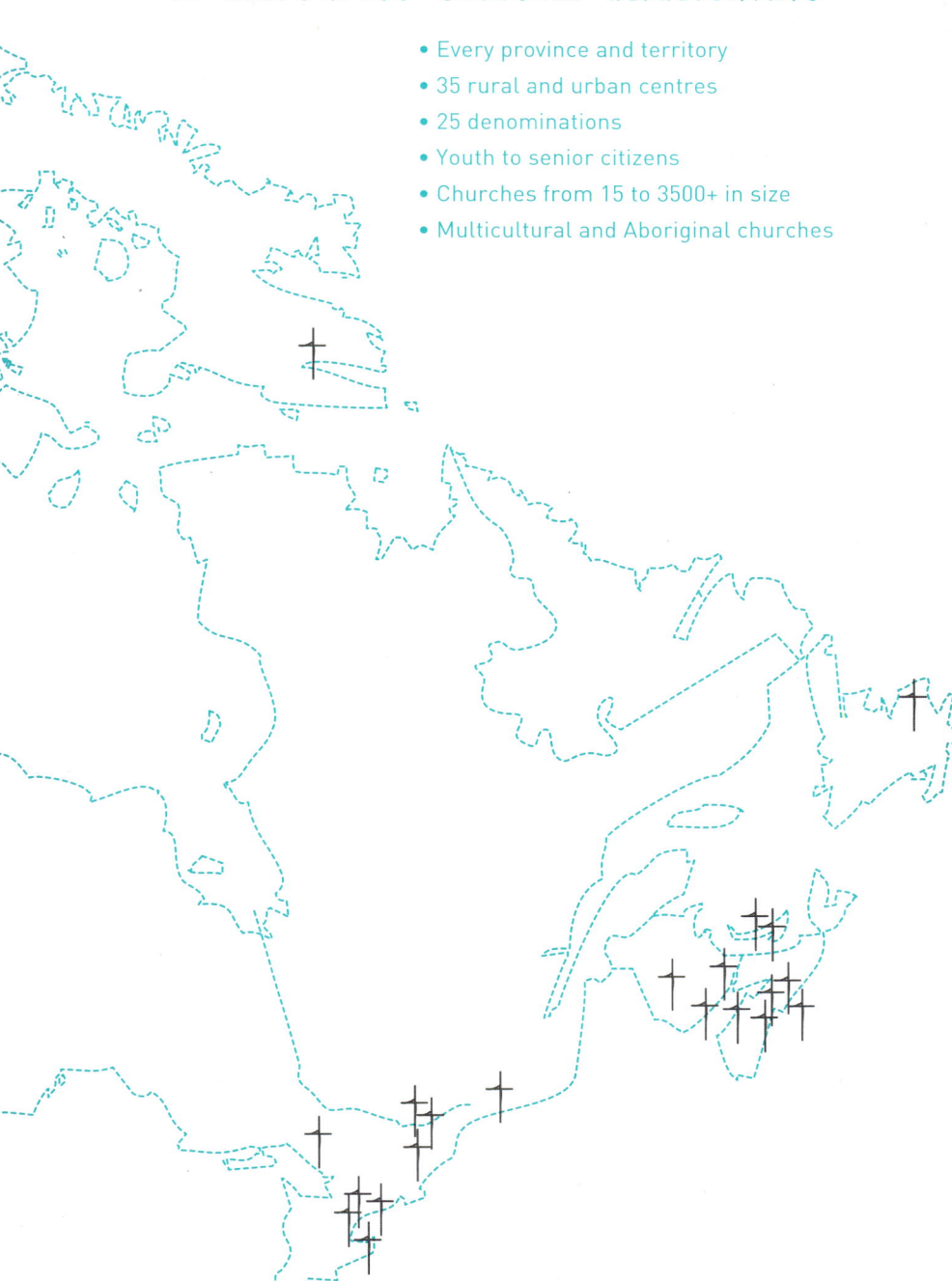

CONTENTS

FOREWORD 1
INTRODUCTION 5

1. NOURISHING STUDENT BODIES—AND SOULS
   Victoria, BC 9

2. UNLEASHING THE POTENTIAL
   OF KIDS IN FREDERICTON
   Fredericton, NB 15

3. OPENING DOORS TO NEW IMMIGRANTS
   Mississauga, ON 21

4. TOUCHING LIVES BY TAPPING SHOULDERS
   Altona, MB 27

5. REACHING THE WEB, REACHING THE WORLD
   Longueuil, QC 35

6. STRENGTHENING FAITH AND ABORIGINAL CULTURE
   Iqaluit, NU 41

7. REFUGEE RELIEF IN SASKATOON
   Saskatoon, SK 47

8. CULTIVATING COMPASSION—CREATING KOINONIA
   Ottawa, ON 53

9. ENGAGING HANDS AND HEARTS IN COMMUNITY
   Lacombe, AB 59

10. RENOVATED ROOMS—AND RESTORED LIVES
    Winnipeg, MB 65

11. A PODCAST CAN CHANGE YOUR WORLD
    Lower Sackville, NS 71

12. IMMIGRANTS: WELCOME TO THE ISLAND
    Charlottetown, PE 77

13. **COACHING AND CONNECTING TO TACKLE DEBT**
    Kemptville, ON 85

14. **ENGAGING YOUTH—BUILDING RELATIONSHIPS**
    Regina, SK 91

15. **STRONG MARRIAGES, STRONG COMMUNITY**
    Richmond, BC 97

16. **WATCHING VOLUNTEERS FLY IN MONCTON**
    Moncton, NB 103

17. **TEXTING FOR TRUTH**
    Calgary, AB 109

18. **MAKING ROOM IN CANADA'S NORTH**
    Whitehorse, YT 115

19. **RESHAPING TRADITION—REVITALIZING YOUTH**
    Halifax, NS 121

20. **PURGE SUNDAYS: INNIES AND OUTIES**
    Oakville, ON 127

21. **EMPOWERING KIDS AND STRENGTHENING FAMILIES**
    Charlottetown, PE 133

22. **ALL IN THE FAMILY**
    Gatineau, QC 139

23. **FURNISHING WITH LOVE IN GANDER**
    Gander, NL 147

24. **IT'S MORE THAN JUST A MEAL**
    Grand Bay, NB 153

25. **MAKING DIGITAL CONNECTIONS**
    Winnipeg, MB 159

26. **JESUS ISN'T ONLY FOR WHITE PEOPLE**
    Abbotsford, BC 165

27. **FLOURISHING FAMILIES AND FRIENDSHIPS**
    North Bay, ON 171

28. **SHOTS AND SWAPS**
    Charlie Lake, BC 177

29. CAMPING IN PARADISE
Hay River, NT 183

30. BECOMING "MIGHTY NEIGHBOURLY"
Chestermere, AB 189

31. DROWNING IN DEBT—LIFTED BY FAITH
Halifax, NS 195

32. MINISTRY IN AN UNEXPECTED PLACE
Vancouver, BC 201

33. SMALL CHURCH—BIG TECH IMPACT
Ajax, ON 207

34. BENEVOLENCE WITHOUT BRANDING
Medicine Hat, AB 213

35. WELCOMING DIVERSITY IN WINNIPEG
Winnipeg, MB 219

36. SINGLE PARENTS: BUILDING BRIDGES
Middleton, NS 225

37. HOW "CHRISTIAN" BECAME MORE THAN JUST A NAME
Lloydminster, SK 231

38. HARVESTING FRUIT AND FRIENDSHIP
St. Catharines, ON 237

39. ADOPTIVE AND FOSTER FAMILIES FINDING HOPE
Calgary, AB 243

40. CRASHING THE TIME CRUNCH
Dartmouth, NS 249

CONCLUSION 255
POSTSCRIPT 265
STORY MATRIX: BY THEME 270
STORY MATRIX: BY REGION 274
STORY MATRIX: BY DENOMINATION 280
STORY MATRIX: BY CHURCH SIZE 287
MEET THE AUTHORS 292

FOREWORD

REV. DR. DON MOORE
National Church Ambassador,
World Vision Canada

Did you know...

• Canada is home to one of the most multi-ethnic, multicultural, multi-religious populations on the planet, with over 200 ethnicities?

• More teens in this country now identify as Muslim than Anglican, United Church of Canada and Baptist—combined?

• Canadians spend more time online than citizens of any other country in the world?

• Household debt levels are at a record level of 163.4 percent, meaning that Canadians spend more than $1.63 for every dollar they make?

Facts and stats like these are the new realities in Canada's rapidly shifting landscape. Many churches across our nation are responding creatively to these changes while others are wrestling with these and other issues in their communities.

We are at a special time in history. What a wonderful opportunity we have to listen and learn from one another as we endeavour to lead in our circles of influence.

This is why it's such a delight to share this book with you. In your hands you hold 40 exceptional stories, each showing a creative church responding to the changing realities across Canada. Really, this is a labour of love: about Canadian churches, for Canadian churches.

Let me paint a picture for you. It's late March in Saskatoon—chilly and grey outdoors, with the hope of spring still far away. But inside a church, 50 or so church leaders have warmed up the sanctuary with animated conversation. Sitting at round tables, the leaders lean toward each other. Several speak excitedly, gesturing with their hands. Others listen, deep in thought. A few pairs have pushed back their chairs for side conversations, talking and nodding vigorously.

This is a snapshot of an inspiring discussion—one of many that took place during our 2014 Annual Church Leaders Forum, Shifting Stats: Shaking the Church. As part of this forum, I visited 10 cities across Canada, meeting more than 800 church leaders.

At these presentations I shared the latest statistics and research from a variety of Canadian sources. Bruxy Cavey, Teaching Pastor at The Meeting House, then talked about how Christians can respond with a compelling Gospel message.

Then, we listened.

We heard stories of struggle and success, of how Canadian congregations of all shapes and sizes, from coast to coast and across denominations are responding to these very real shifts in Canadian society.

Not only did folks discuss these issues at their tables, but at each of our forums we asked leaders to write down names of churches that were following God in responding to these shifting stats. In addition, I asked denominational leaders with whom I met to identify their own churches that are in step with a changing Canada.

Together, we received more than 200 inspiring leads. We commissioned journalists Patricia Paddey and Karen Stiller to pursue the final stories. We also identified and asked ministry specialists to offer their insights—you'll see them quoted in the sidebars throughout.

This book is a tour into the hearts, minds and daily lives of ordinary Canadian congregations ministering in extraordinary times. It represents many parts of the body of Christ. As I read it, I'm reminded of this beautiful passage from 1 Corinthians 12: 12-13 (NIV): "Just as a body, though one, has many parts, but all its many parts form one body, so it is with Christ. For we were all baptized by one Spirit so as to form one body."

We hope you'll be inspired by these stories. May this book challenge us all to consider the shifting stats of the Canadian landscape, and to respond with grace, truth and creativity—for the sake of His Kingdom and His glory!

INTRODUCTION

Stats are not the only things shifting. The Church in Canada is also changing.

The Church is changing in response to statistically measurable shifts in Canadian society and culture, and the needs and opportunities for ministry that those shifts present.

This is not news: Christianity has always been shaped by the surrounding culture. Regent College theologian John Stackhouse says that the challenge for Canadian churches today remains what it has always been, that is, "to connect with the felt needs of our neighbours."

If you have lived in this country for any amount of time you've no doubt seen those "felt needs" shift as Canadian culture itself has undergone a transformation. Some of the most obvious changes have occurred in: the ethnic, cultural and religious composition of the population; the structure of Canadian families; the needs of youth; the ways people use their time (including their willingness and availability to volunteer); the ways Canadians use their money; and finally, the enormous differences in our everyday lives brought about by new technologies.

If you worship or serve in one of Canada's many thousands of congregations—professionally or as a layperson—you know this shifting reality well. You've lived it, perhaps delighted in it, been worried or saddened by it. Maybe you've even lost sleep over it.

As journalists who have devoted years to documenting stories in and about the Canadian Church, and as individuals who have benefitted from—and participated in—the life of the Church in myriad ways (Karen is a clergy spouse and Patricia a seminary student), we share your joys, frustrations and concerns.

We were born in the '60s. We remember a time when the Church operated at the centre of Canadian culture, when people who did not affiliate with a church were the exception. We remember reciting the Lord's Prayer in our public schools and hearing secular leaders invoke God—boldly and unashamedly—in public spaces.

Within our lifetimes, we've been witnesses to the cultural shifts that have resulted in the Church being moved incrementally but increasingly to the margins of our society.

But being at the margins may not be the worst place for the Church to be. As writer Anne Lamott has noted, it is at the margins, "where so many juicy moments of life and spirit and friendship" can be found.

It was with an attitude of searching out some of the juiciest moments occurring in and through churches—across the country and across denominations—that we embarked on a journey of discovery, the results of which you'll find narrated in the pages that follow.

At the outset of this project, we expected to find that there were churches in our country that are struggling or, worse, stagnating. But we also trusted there were many, many congregations responding to the individual needs of their unique communities in innovative ways.

Our goal in rooting out and relating the 40 stories that follow has been to work with World Vision Canada in their desire to create an effective and helpful resource that will serve to inform, inspire, encourage and motivate the Church we love.

Christians believe God created human beings in His image, to represent Him in creation. That means all humanity has an important part to play in making God's world what it is supposed to be. But as believers, we have an additional responsibility because Christ, who lives in us, calls us to proclaim his Gospel.

This book contains evidence that the Canadian Church in 2014 is proclaiming the truth of the Gospel confidently—in both word and deed. You'll find true stories about churches from sea to sea to sea, from 25 different denominational affiliations, with an average Sunday attendance from as small as 15 to as large as 3500.

The stories focus on how churches are responding to specific changes in the areas of immigration, the family, youth, volunteering and Canadians' use of finances, time and money.

Each story illuminates a single church in a single community responding to the changing needs of the changing society around it. In so doing, each one is carrying out a piece of the universal Church's larger mission, the scope of which missiologist Michael Goheen describes as being "as broad as creation, because God's mission is the redemption of the whole world."

As journalists, we have long believed that every person has a story worth telling. On these pages we proclaim our conviction that every church has one too.

As you read about these 40 churches, take time to linger over the "More to Explore" points at the end of each chapter. They are there for your consideration and for further reflection. Some of these points are statistics gleaned during the course of our research, while others are conclusions we have drawn as a result of working to understand and tell that particular church's story.

Writing in the book of Romans the apostle Paul calls his readers to understand the times, to behave accordingly, and to live honourably (Romans 13:11–13). Two thousand years later and half a world away, it is no less critical for Canadian Christians to understand our own cultural context, to respond appropriately and to live with integrity within this context.

May the stories in this book help and encourage us all to do exactly that.

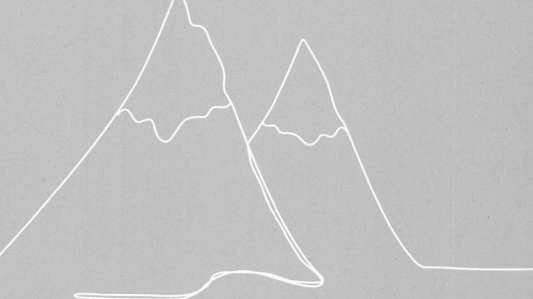

VICTORIA, BRITISH COLUMBIA

NOURISHING STUDENT BODIES—AND SOULS

1. NOURISHING STUDENT BODIES —AND SOULS

Every Tuesday, from September to April, an exodus happens at the University of Victoria (UVic) in British Columbia.

By the hundreds, students make their way on foot across campus and then across the mature, tree-lined street to the promised land: Emmanuel Baptist Church. Some have a faith background—Christian or otherwise—while others would describe themselves as "religion: none at all." They come solo, in twos and threes, or in packs. They come for a single hour or for several. But all are lured by the promise of milk and honey. The church calls it "Student Dinner."

For more than a decade, Emmanuel's congregation has extended a weekly welcome to UVic students throughout the academic year, providing a place for quiet study, regular respite from the rigours of university life, an opportunity to gather with old friends and meet new ones, and plenty of delicious, home-cooked food. It's all served up with casual friendliness, warm hospitality and a genuine "no strings attached" policy.

What began in 2004 as a dinner for a dozen students, hosted by a few volunteers with a vision to build trusting relationships with the UVic community, has burgeoned into regular hospitality and care for some 450 young adults from the campus across the street throughout the fall and spring semesters.

"We estimate we've served more than 67,000 meals over the years," says Catherine Scambler who with her husband Paul coordinates the Student Dinner ministry. Together, they oversee some 80 volunteers and the weekly gathering, preparation and distribution of enough food to ensure no one leaves hungry. They both consider the endeavour as ongoing testimony to the provision of God, a provision that, to the casual observer, seems no less miraculous than the feeding of the 5000.

"Students start to arrive at the church usually by midday," says Paul. "They come to use the room as a study space. We make Wi-Fi available. Coffee is offered from about 4 p.m. onwards." So is Mozart. "One study claims it inspires intellectual activity," quips Catherine.

By 5 p.m. all of the tables are occupied to some degree, and within another half-hour all 270 seats are usually taken. The meal is served in two sittings, with the first beginning at 6 p.m.

Two long lines of buffet tables—heavily laden with fresh bread, salads, casseroles, roast chicken, pasta, potatoes, vegetarian dishes, vegan options and desserts—beckon rows of hungry students on each side. The Scamblers calculate a student ambles away from the buffet tables every eight seconds. When everyone has been through the buffet once, they are invited to go back for second helpings. Students bring their own plastic containers to fill with leftovers to take home; at the end of the evening free bread is given out to any student who wants it, courtesy of a local bakery. Students leave when they must—some have to run off to evening classes—but the evening officially wraps up around 7:30 p.m.

The menu is always slightly different; there are no sign-up sheets for volunteers, so whatever the congregation (and a few local businesses) happen to contribute each week is what the students eat. But there has always been a good variety. And there has always been enough. This is a potluck of plenty.

"I first went in 2010," says Nicole Morgan, a recent UVic graduate who quickly became a regular at the gatherings. Her one regret about leaving school is missing out on Church Dinner.

She first heard about the weekly offering through the friend of a friend and only hesitated about going she says, because, "I don't identify with any religion. But once I had gone, I realized they're not out to force anything on you. They say grace every meal. But I just felt really comfortable, really early."

> IT WAS WONDERFUL TO HAVE THE FEELING THAT PEOPLE WERE LOOKING OUT FOR YOU. THAT PEOPLE CARED.

Emmanuel volunteers work hard to cultivate that kind of comfortable atmosphere every week. A prayer team—out of sight, in another room—prays for the students throughout the meal. Blank paper and coloured markers on each table encourage students to play hangman or leave behind doodles, messages or even prayer requests. Large tubs of board games offer distractions from studying, and open mic nights each term allow students to display their wit and talent.

A carefully crafted vision statement—visible to students and volunteers alike—helps to keep intentions transparent and the Emmanuel team focused: "Motivated by the love of Jesus, the vision of the student dinners is to build trusting relationships with students through faithful demonstrations of hospitality and care, with no strings attached."

The Scamblers have observed notable changes in the profile of students who have come over the past decade. There are far more international students now. Students now have greater financial needs: some regularly depend on the local food bank to feed themselves, and many have said Church Dinner is their one good meal a week.

A recent note from a student captures the reality of living on a student budget: "I have 10 dollars and 27 cents in the bank account," the student wrote. "Thank you for filling my belly."

Catherine concedes it's been a challenge at times to secure enough volunteers within Emmanuel's aging congregation and to cover the annual $8,000 dinner costs within the church budget. Providing the free weekly meal is not about proselytization, nor about reaching out to the poor. It's also "not just hospitality," says Catherine. "It's mission. We form a part of the whole Church, and we're building trust with students, which is doing a small piece of the Church's larger mission."

Young people have come through the doors initially distrusting, or even hostile towards Christianity. They've left with a far more positive attitude, having encountered people who made it clear their only motive was to care and to serve.

"It was really the highlight of my week," says Nicole. "I loved going. The food was fantastic. For a student who's far away from home, it was wonderful to have the feeling that people were looking out for you. That people cared. That there was always someone you could talk to if you needed to."

EMMANUEL BAPTIST CHURCH
2121 Cedar Hill Cross Road, Victoria, BC | Ph. 250.592.2418
www.emmanuelvictoria.ca

MORE TO EXPLORE

 As costs of post-secondary education in this country continue to escalate, a free, "no strings attached" meal can be a welcome gift and a way of building relationship with cash-strapped students.

 According to Statistics Canada, "religiosity is lowest among young people." *Canadian Social Trends*, Summer 2006, No. 81. **www.publications.gc.ca**

 Recent generations of Canadians are significantly less affiliated to religious institutions than earlier generations. *Canada's Changing Religious Landscape*. **www.pewforum.org**

 According to the recent 'Hemorrhaging Faith' study, "There is a strange paradox that arises when it comes to young adults and community. The emerging generation is fiercely independent and self-reliant. Yet its members say there's nothing more important to them than friendship. They crave relationship and long for a place of belonging." Penner, James, Rachel Harder, Erika Anderson, Bruno Desourcy and Rick Hiemstra. 'Hemorrhaging Faith: Why and When Canadian Young Adults are Leaving, Staying and Returning to Church'. Toronto: EFC Youth and Young Adult Ministry Roundtable, 2013.
www.tgcfcanada.org/hemorrhagingfaith

FREDERICTON, NEW BRUNSWICK

UNLEASHING THE POTENTIAL
OF KIDS IN FREDERICTON

2. UNLEASHING THE POTENTIAL OF KIDS IN FREDERICTON

Twelve-year-old Max Goodine of Fredericton, New Brunswick has never read a leadership book, but he has some pretty clear ideas about what leadership entails.

"A leader is a servant. I mean, Jesus came and washed people's feet," says Max. "You should go with a humble heart. A leader is someone who is doing something people can't do, either for them or with them. You are a guide for people too, to help them in the right way."

A well-spoken and confident young man, Max says his definition of leadership was both "confirmed and expanded" through his experience with Kid LEAD, an unabashedly hardcore leadership-training program for kids offered through his church, Smythe Street Cathedral.

They call it a boot camp—and they're not kidding. "We push their limits with things like rock climbing or zip lining," explains Heidi Billington, family ministries director for Smythe Street. She is a maker of leaders and the brains behind Camp Lead, the weeklong summer camp that immerses kids from ages nine to 13 in the Bible and in leadership development through learning and doing. "The first year we focused more on virtues, the second year on specific people from the Bible. It was a Bible Olympics in a way. They had massive amounts of homework at night."

This is not a Vacation Bible School (VBS)—although if you attend Camp Lead you are expected to serve at the church's VBS. The special summer camp is a precursor to the leadership training that continues one Sunday a month through the year, building on the summer's lessons—and catapulting kids normally kept in the background to front and centre and increasingly responsible leadership positions in the life of the church.

Camp Lead is a time for kids to discover their skills—like the girl who realized her talent for creating beautiful things. "To think," says Heidi, "that she might have sat through crafts being taught to her for the next two or three years is just ridiculous." Instead, the girl led crafts at VBS. "She really blew our socks off," says Heidi.

Excursions into the community give kids hands-on experience in service. The kid-leaders have made maple syrup at a local Christian treatment centre for men with addictions. "We helped them and talked about how hard work is vital to being a leader and a good citizen," says Heidi. They've visited hospitals: "We had one little guy who was a natural. He didn't know the ability he had to speak to people. He was so moved by the experience he went home and told his mom, 'Maybe this is what God put me on the earth for.'"

The kids have built sets for Christmas plays. The youth may be called to help with ushering and announcements or other duties in a Sunday service. And the budding leaders are always welcome into the Volunteer Café at the church, a special coffee nook set aside for volunteers. Kids love that feeling of being part of a special group with privileges, says Heidi.

"Their confidence changes. As these kids head into the most hormonally-infused, tumultuous period of their lives, to set them up as who they are in Christ is so essential," she says. "We present it like an internship. You can do all the study you want but until you are hands-on, working on it, you don't feel the ownership," Heidi explains. "We want these kids to feel that touching their community is something they are called to. And not when they are 30, but when they are 13."

This conviction to unleash the leadership potential in kids now, not later, came to Heidi at 40,000 feet, flying home from a World Vision trip to Haiti. She had been a few times—her first trip landing in Port-au-Prince just two hours before the disastrous earthquake of January 2010.

"Our hearts were instantly connected with Haiti in a way we didn't anticipate," says Heidi. That connection would grow during two subsequent visits as Smythe Street solidified their links with a Haitian community through a World Vision pilot project that linked Fredericton with Haiti. Heidi began to notice something about the children she was meeting in Haiti. Their leadership skills startled her. They were not being spoon-fed church programs; they led the programs.

> WE WANT THESE KIDS TO FEEL THAT TOUCHING THEIR COMMUNITY IS SOMETHING THEY ARE CALLED TO, AND NOT WHEN THEY ARE 30, BUT WHEN THEY ARE 13.

"God was saying to me: 'You give your life back home to partner with parents and raise children up spiritually in the ways of God, but you've missed out on this component of leadership and assumed that children need things done for them,'" says Heidi. "I watched these young men and women stand up and introduce the projects. They are so articulate and can lead music, but back at home we are doing it all for the children."

How dare we invest in this way in Haiti and not carry that investment home, thought Heidi. So she did. She raised the bar and raised some eyebrows. "Every time I raise it a little higher, I get this skeptical look, but they always do it. We are all surprised by what they are capable of. I believe our congregation is being won over by surprise in what God is doing with ones so young."

Theresa Goodine is Max's mom. She has definitely been won over. "I've seen Max mature in his leadership skills. He thrives at it. It brings the very best out in him. If he was just being told to sit in a chair and to listen, he would not be excelling—he would be bored," says Theresa. "They have to learn who they are meant to be now. They're not just going to be suddenly a giving and caring person."

For Max, it is, quite simply, cool. "They always say to train young people in the way they should go," reflects Max. "I think it's cool they are doing that. And I get to be a part of it."

> "Jesus said 'Where your treasure is there your heart will be also.' We all care about what we've invested in. Churches should be asking 'What opportunities have we given our youth to invest here with their time, talents and treasures?'"
>
> **– Rick Hiemstra**,
> Head of Research for the Evangelical Fellowship of Canada, co-author of *Hemorrhaging Faith*

SMYTHE STREET CATHEDRAL
913 Smythe Street, Fredericton, NB | Ph. 506.458.8206
www.smythestreetcathedral.com

MORE TO EXPLORE

 FreddyLink is the name of the pilot project linking Fredericton with Haiti through World Vision Canada. Smythe Street Cathedral is a partner, along with other community groups. Learn more at **www.freddylink.com**.

 World Vision offers global partnership opportunities that you can learn more about at **www.churches.worldvision.ca**

 In 'Hemorrhaging Faith: Why & When Canadian Young Adults are Leaving, Staying & Returning to Church', the authors report the following points of interest about leadership and youth in the church:

1. "Engagers" (or those youth who remain in the Church) were the most likely to say they had been offered opportunities to lead in the Church.

2. Youth who have mostly ceased to attend religious services were the least likely to have experienced leadership opportunities in the Church.

3. Young adults who believe their talents were not appreciated in the Church are less likely to attend.
www.tgcfcanada.org/hemorrhagingfaith

3. OPENING DOORS TO NEW IMMIGRANTS

Ask Pastor Julius Tiangson ("PJ" to his congregants at Gateway Church and to hundreds—if not thousands—of Canadian immigrants) what the Gateway Centre for New Canadians does particularly well, and he doesn't need a moment to think about it. "Youth and seniors," he says.

The seniors are obvious on this weekday morning. Dozens of mostly Chinese and Filipino seniors are line dancing in one of the Centre's wood-floored studios. Hips swaying, legs kicking, shoulders dipping, they respond to the rhythms of the music and commands of a petite Asian woman wearing an over-the-ear-and-around-the-cheek microphone: "Five, six, seven, eight! Kick-ball-chain!"

Gateway is not now, nor has it ever been, a typical church. Launched in 2000 as a Filipino church plant of the Christian and Missionary Alliance Church in Canada, today's Gateway shelters under the umbrella of Church Planting Ministries Inc. Gateway's growing network of followers of Jesus has never offered traditional church programming or built a church building. From the start, they've poured their resources into this 25,000-square-foot community centre located in the heart of Canada's sixth largest city, Mississauga, Ontario.

A not-for-profit corporation, the Gateway Centre for New Canadians opened its doors in July 2004. Those doors have remained open thanks to a combination of government funding, program fees and public and private partnerships. The Centre houses the space where the congregation meets for weekly worship. It is a place for newcomers to the city to get introduced to the church as they find support in the form of language and skills training, as well as settlement, family, business, health and recreation services. Since its inception, the Centre has bustled. There are plenty of newcomers in Mississauga: according to recent Census data, just over half the population of this city is foreign-born.

The church's mission statement—"To become the greatest expression of God's limitless goodness"—has been the driving force behind an innovative approach to ministry, rooted in mentoring seekers and channeling them into small groups.

Some more traditionally-minded believers have sometimes felt uncomfortable. "When you begin to attract people from all different faith backgrounds," begins Tiangson, "well, I've even doubted myself."

When Tiangson agreed to allow a Muslim group to rent space in the Centre for Friday prayer meetings in 2007, "I lost 60 percent of my congregation," he says without flinching. "Three-quarters of my leadership left." Yet he insists he has no regrets, that he refuses to "pamper" longtime believers and would rather direct his energies toward people who don't yet know Jesus. The Muslims have stayed, and Tiangson has been a frequent guest at their prayer meetings, where he's been invited to speak of his relationship with "Isa" (Jesus).

Those of many other faith backgrounds—and of no faith at all—have also continued to come.

In more than a decade of operation, Tiangson, a handful of staff and hundreds of volunteers have ministered to people of 36 different nationalities and all ages. Between 500 and 1000 people use Gateway's various programs and services each week.

Fredie Buen first came to the Gateway Centre for New Canadians in 2008 at the age of 22. "I was really just looking for a place to dance for free," he says. "I started to dance at 13. It's always been a liberating way to express myself. It meant the world to me."

> THE CHURCH'S MISSION STATEMENT, "TO BECOME THE GREATEST EXPRESSION OF GOD'S LIMITLESS GOODNESS," HAS... LEFT SOME MORE TRADITIONALLY-MINDED BELIEVERS FEELING UNCOMFORTABLE.

Fredie is a first generation Filipino-Canadian who was a troubled young man when he first came to the Centre for hip-hop. He'd done jail time for armed robbery, and had struggled with heroin addiction. But there was something about the Christ-centred "I Rock with the ONE" hip-hop dance program at Gateway that attracted him. So much so that he endured five-hour commutes (taking three trains, then three buses) to get there during rush-hour traffic, five or six days each week.

"The whole God thing has always been pretty rough for me," he says. "I got into a lot of trouble growing up." But eight months into his engagement with Gateway's unique dance program, "I told God I was sorry for how I'd been leading my life. I dropped to my knees and cried."

Today, Fredie is a husband and father. He has his own painting business, which offers employment opportunities to youth. Weekends and evenings, he runs a Christ-centred, award-winning Tae Kwon Do youth outreach program at Gateway called "Limitless Tae Kwon Do." (He earned his black belt before he started to dance.) "It's my ministry," he says, "My way of giving back to Gateway."

These days, Tiangson talks about plans to establish a Gateway credit union, set up an accelerated home-ownership program for would-be home owners, and to open a daycare and a Montessori school within the building.

Meantime, the church congregation—95 percent of whom, Tiangson estimates, come from non-church backgrounds—will continue to pursue their mission through what they call an "F-6 life plan," focusing on faith, family, finance, fitness and fun, fulfillment and "followership."

Gesturing broadly to the building around him, Tiangson says the Gateway Centre was "born of God." But the birth has come through a long and painful labour. Still, Tiangson holds firmly to his conviction of the need for a systematic way of reaching immigrants so that they will come to know and understand the love of Christ.

THE GATEWAY CENTRE
3450 Wolfedale Road, Mississauga, ON | Ph. 905.848.1106
www.mygatewaycentre.org

MORE TO EXPLORE

 Through the creative use of public, private and community partnerships, what began as a small, mono-ethnic congregation has been able to build a Christ-centred ministry that serves newcomers to Canada of all ages.

 Canada is home to one of the most multi-ethnic, multicultural, multi-religious populations on the planet. Our population is composed of more than 200 different ethnicities according to Citizenship and Immigration Canada's annual report on the 'Operation of the Canadian Multiculturalism' Act 2011–2012: Promoting Integration. **www.cic.gc.ca**

 More teens in this country now identify as Muslim than Anglican, United Church of Canada and Baptist combined. Lunau, Kate. "Youth Survey: Teens lose faith in droves." *Maclean's*, April 7, 2009. **www.macleans.ca**

TOUCHING LIVES BY TAPPING SHOULDERS

4. TOUCHING LIVES BY TAPPING SHOULDERS

It just might be every pastor's dream: a church of 500 souls, situated in a lovely little town of only 4000. Especially when that town is Altona.

Located in southern Manitoba, Altona has been called an oasis on the prairies. And for good reason: the sweet smell of country air here is accompanied by an abundance of sunshine. Indeed, the sun reportedly shines on Altona for more hours every year than in any other region in Canada.

But it's more than fresh air, broad blue skies and sunny days that have helped to give this place its reputation as a refuge. Altona is a community founded by immigrants. Beginning in the early 1870s, German-speaking Mennonites fleeing persecution in Russia came in waves, attracted by the promise of fertile soil and religious freedom.

Today, the congregation of Altona Evangelical Mennonite Mission Church (EMMC), while growing more diverse, is still largely composed of the descendants of those first oasis-seekers. Names like Friesen and Klassen, Thiessen and Driedger figure prominently in the rolls.

The town continues to be a safe haven for refugees and an attractive first destination for new immigrants today. Perhaps compassion comes more easily when you understand what someone else is going through because you've been there yourself.

Altona EMMC has had little difficulty enlisting volunteers to help newcomers integrate into Canadian life, says Ben Klassen, Pastor of Teaching and Discipleship. "We have a very strong volunteer base in our church," he explains. "We don't do a lot of pushing from the pulpit to get volunteers. It's much more a tapping-on-shoulders and inviting people into [service]."

Large numbers of people serve both in the church and in the community as an expression of worship to God. Inside the church, there are plenty of opportunities to serve: Sunday school and youth ministry, worship teams, mid-week clubs for children, a young moms' Bible study, mentoring programs and ministry to women and seniors. The church also has a well-established prison ministry and a food services ministry that prepares and coordinates meals for everything from church family dinners to funerals.

But it is the church's ministry to refugees that Klassen describes as an effort arising "from the grassroots."

Members of Altona EMMC joined with members from several other community churches to form a non-profit organization called "Build A Village." Build A Village sponsors one or two refugee families every other year.

The refugees come from places like Sudan, Burundi, Rwanda, Syria and Iraq. Many are Muslim. Many have experienced terrible trauma in the countries they've fled. They arrive with little, and once here, they need financial support, as well as help in locating housing and jobs, acquiring language, enrolling their children in schools, and generally integrating into the community. The needs of the immigrant community become opportunities for this Christian community to serve.

Of course, "there are a lot of pressures on people that would cause them to not volunteer," Klassen concedes. "Economic pressures, family pressures, just the basic pressures of our world." But a few years ago, Klassen sensed that Jesus' parable of the sheep and the goats (Matthew 25: 31–46) had captured the imaginations of the congregation. He doesn't remember preaching about the parable. He just became aware that people were talking about it—in conversations and email messages—and concluded the story "has been a very key passage in driving a lot of people into volunteering."

As people began to see that in serving "the least of these" in their community, they were serving Christ, Klassen says, "It's shaped what we do in prisons and our immigrant programs, both of which are key ministries of our church."

The immigrant programs Klassen refers to are Hopes and Dreams and English Café, two innovative outreach initiatives designed to meet the needs of newcomers to Canada.

"Hopes and Dreams is a program we run each spring," he explains. "It's designed to help immigrants reach their hopes and dreams for life in Canada."

Hopes and Dreams picks up where English as a Second Language (ESL) classes leave off. In 2010, Klassen's wife Cindy was teaching ESL. She saw firsthand the disappointment of her students when they realized classes took a break from April until September. "When faced with this gap, they were like, 'Really? We're done? What are we going to do now?'" she recalls.

Thanks to Hopes and Dreams, what they do now is sit down with church volunteers who take the time to ask them about their goals. Those volunteers then set out to provide the needed support to help immigrant families achieve their aspirations. Dreams have involved everything from earning a driver's license to seeing children succeed in school, from learning how to cook "Canadian" to just having good friends.

"If it means taking someone driving that's what we do," says Val Klassen, who co-coordinates the program (which runs Monday evenings from April to June) with her husband Gary. He describes the program as being, "really quite activity-based."

The goal is to get the community together. Sometimes women will do crafts or have a cooking class, visit a local farm or garden centre. The men might play soccer. Volunteers expose the children to typical Canadian childhood pursuits, like playing baseball or blowing bubbles.

English Café runs on Monday evenings from September to April. It matches volunteers one-to-one with people who come to sit, enjoy a cup of coffee and share conversation with the simple goal of practising their English language skills.

"Over and over again, we're reminded by our newcomers how much relationships are important to them," says Val. "And that's been humbling. We tend to be far more task-oriented. But they're interested in just getting to know you and spending time with you."

> WE DON'T DO A LOT OF PUSHING FROM THE PULPIT TO GET VOLUNTEERS. IT'S MUCH MORE A TAPPING-ON-SHOULDERS AND INVITING PEOPLE INTO SERVICE.

Amal Abueraiban came to Canada from Jordan in 2010 with her husband and eight children. She says it has meant a great deal to her to meet new friends. "First when I came I was shy," she remembers. "But when I came to Hopes and Dreams and English Café, it gave me opportunity to make friends and talk together. The volunteers became my friends. We learn together about each other's culture."

Abueraiban says receiving help with her ESL homework, and having a place where she can ask questions has been helpful. But more importantly, she says the volunteers "are my friends. We meet to have tea together in their homes. It helps me not to be lonely."

The Klassens have found the necessary volunteers through a lot of shoulder tapping.

"One woman—we tapped her on the shoulder and said, 'Hey, have you ever thought of being involved?'" says Val. "She came twice, and then we asked her if she would like to coordinate snacks. And she thought that was where she best fit."

Maria Reimer is that woman. She enlists others to bake or prepare snacks. Then each Monday, she arrives early, starts the coffee, and sets out the dishes and food. "I love it," she enthuses. "I enjoy meeting new people, and this is a nice thing to do."

Val and Gary Klassen say their lives are also richer for the friendships they've developed through their volunteer efforts. "Your life and my life flow into each other as wave flows into wave," Gary says, quoting Frederick Buechner, "and unless there is peace and joy and freedom for you, there can be no real peace or joy or freedom for me."

Concluding the quote he pauses, then adds, "We want this peace and joy and freedom for everybody."

Cindy Klassen is thoughtful when asked about the impact that volunteering has had on the people of Altona EMMC. "No matter who we are, we want to make a difference. We want our lives to matter.

"As Christians we know it's also a calling on our life. And then when you see other people succeed because you were there for them, you see them driving around town and you hear their English improve year after year, you feel good about the part you've played in that. It's a joy to have your life matter."

> "Our North American concept of 'community' is not nearly as deep and warm as many of the communities from which our refugee friends come. Hence our churches can also feel cold and superficial. We really have to make a significant effort to meaningfully reach out or we will lose them."
>
> – **Anne Woolger**, Founder and Director, Matthew House, Toronto.

ALTONA EVANGELICAL MENNONITE MISSION CHURCH
158 2nd Street NE, Altona, MB | Ph. 204.324.8432
www.emmc.altona.mb.ca

MORE TO EXPLORE

 At Altona EMMC, church leaders have adopted a soft, tap-on-the-shoulder approach rather than a hard-sell, pitch-from-the-pulpit for volunteers. Ministry leaders prayerfully consider who might be a good fit for a volunteer role, then approach that individual and ask them to consider becoming involved.

 Jesus' parable of the sheep and the goats (as told in Matthew 25) has served as significant inspiration to the congregation, motivating individuals and helping to shape ministries.

 Almost half of all Canadians over the age of 15 (47 percent) contributed their time, energy and skills to groups and organizations such as charities and nonprofits as volunteers in 2010. That represents an increase in the rate of volunteerism of 6.4 percent over 2007, and 12.5 percent over 2004.

Vezina, Mireille and Susan Crompton. "Volunteering in Canada." *Canadian Social Trends*, Component of Statistics Canada Catalogue no. 11-008-X, April 16, 2012.
www.statcan.gc.ca

LONGUEUIL, QUEBEC

REACHING THE WEB,
REACHING THE WORLD

5. REACHING THE WEB, REACHING THE WORLD

The lovely Alice Pomerleau settles herself into a large brown leather chair in a darkened room. "My name is Alice Pomerleau. This is my story," she begins.

What follows is an eight-minute and fifteen-second account, in French, of Pomerleau's journey through the anguish of anorexia. Her voice is clear and strong. She gestures with her hands as she speaks, explaining her search for an unconditional kind of love. She tells of the moment of freedom when she found her identity in a relationship with Jesus Christ.

"It was the only thing I was certain of in my life, at this moment. That Jesus loves me. I felt that it was the truth." The video ends with the young woman standing up again: "I am Alice Pomerleau. And that was my story." *Je suis Alice Pomerleau. Et c'était mon histoire.*

Pomerleau's story is part of a "This is my Story" video series produced by the creative technology team of Église Nouvelle Vie.

The church's address may be 200 rue du Parc Industriel, Longueuil, Quebec, but this is a church that equally and intentionally lives out its mission online. They have 11,000 Facebook followers (as of now). Their church's app—a link to the services posted online and the church's schedule—has been downloaded 18,000 times, leading to 750,000 page visits from the app. Nouvelle Vie averages 300,000 annual visitors to their website, usually more than 800 a day. And those visits come from 168 different countries. When Alice's video hit the site—part of a short series by young women who had suffered with anorexia—daily traffic doubled to 1600 for a time.

The video clearly hit a nerve. And Nouvelle Vie has hit its stride with technology.

Nouvelle Vie was never afraid to experiment, spending time developing radio shows years ago. Then they made a conscious choice to zero in on their online potential, committing time and resources to their digital identity. "I heard that the third or fourth largest country in the world was Facebook," explains Jocelyn Olivier, assistant to the senior pastor. "We decided it was time for us to go there and reach people all over the world."

This is a large francophone, evangelical church, probably "one of the largest French churches outside of Africa," says Olivier. "We've been pretty much the leader in many ways." Olivier believes their already existing reputation certainly helps their online offerings spread so abundantly and widely, but so do the facts that the content is free and it is excellent. "Our speakers are often artists and speakers well known in France. Of course, being one of the main French-speaking churches is helping us be known worldwide."

Matthieu Layes is Nouvelle Vie's webmaster. "I think the main feature that drives people to the site is the messages. It's what makes the website popular." The weekly sermons have been posted online for a few years now. As traffic to the site increased, so did the amount of material the church posted online. "The church leadership decided to put every series on the web. That's what leads most people to come to the site," says Layes. At first it was just audio recordings of the sermons. When they switched to video, Layes says the impact was "amazing. The traffic probably doubled in one or two years."

Content is the secret, says Stéphane Hoareau, Director of Communications for the church. "People just come and enjoy the message. Content is the key to the traffic."

That, and ongoing maintenance. Maintaining a website is like gardening: water and weed it so it will grow.

> I HEARD THAT THE THIRD OR FOURTH LARGEST COUNTRY IN THE WORLD WAS FACEBOOK. WE DECIDED IT WAS TIME FOR US TO GO THERE AND REACH PEOPLE ALL OVER THE WORLD.

"If you just leave a page and don't take care of it, it will grow organically but very slowly," says Layes. "It doesn't grow rapidly if you don't take care of it." Posting the weekly message is the first stop in Layes' routine. "First on the website, then on Facebook." He crafts a strong, catchy sentence from the message to introduce the video. "That is one of the strategies. Putting something that is relevant to people like: 'Are you struggling with depression? Look at this message and share it,'" explains Layes. "During the week I will also try and take some key elements from the messages and create images and put them online for people to share. It's usually an encouraging word or sometimes a verse." He strives to post an online update every two or three days.

Nouvelle Vie attempts to stay ahead of technology shifts, rather than running after a bus that has already left the station. Two years ago they began to rebuild the website to ensure it would work well on mobile devices—what opens quickly and works smoothly on a desktop does not always do the same on a smartphone or tablet. "The biggest feature of the new site was a responsive design," says Layes. "No matter the device you use, the website will fit. It's also very efficient for sharing features on Facebook." He notes the trend that Facebook is most often accessed on a mobile device. "When you see a story and a message on Facebook and you want to share it and you land on a page that is not optimized for it, the sharing is limited," he says.

Nouvelle Vie has thrown open its arms and embraced technology "as a way to spread the message," says Stéphane Hoareau. "We look at other churches that are inspiring us, and we are inspired by other churches. It is not just the technology for the sake of doing it. It is to spread the message."

ÉGLISE NOUVELLE VIE
200 rue du Parc Industriel, Longueuil, QC | Ph. 450.646.2150
www.nouvellevie.com

SHIFTING STATS

MORE TO EXPLORE

 56 percent of Canadians have a smartphone and are increasingly reliant on them for a significant amount of their daily transactions, according to a 2013 Google report with Ipsos MediaCT.
www.services.google.com/fh/files/misc/omp-2013-ca-en.pdf

 89 percent of smartphone users look for local information on their phone and 88 percent take action based on that information. One can assume that looking for a church is part of that activity.

 According to its own first quarter 2014 report, Facebook is now the second largest "country" in the world by population. If current growth trends continue, it will surpass China to become number one by 2016.

IQALUIT, NUNAVUT

STRENGTHENING FAITH
AND ABORIGINAL CULTURE

6. STRENGTHENING FAITH AND ABORIGINAL CULTURE

This is a story that involves not a sole church, but several. It encompasses not one single community, but a vast expanse of millions of kilometres across Nunavut and Northern Quebec. It takes place where the Northern Lights dance, but tree branches don't (there are no trees here, north of the tree line), and the total population, widely dispersed, is counted in tens rather than hundreds of thousands.

Ultimately, it is also a story about family, and of how the Church—a family itself—while caring for its own also cared for a language and a culture.

It was a brisk, sunny spring day in June 2012 when hundreds of people gathered at St. Jude's Anglican Cathedral in Iqaluit to celebrate a cultural milestone, the arrival of the Bible in the Inuktitut language.

The Inuktitut Bible—written in syllabics—was a monumental work that took almost three-and-a-half decades to complete. A partnership project of the Canadian Bible Society and the Anglican Church Diocese of the Arctic, translation began in 1978 after the church approached the Bible Society for help producing a Bible in Inuktitut.

Four indigenous priests—Reverend Benjamin Arreak, Reverend Jonas Allooloo, Reverend Andrew Atagotaaluk and Reverend James Nashak—were Inuk men who were selected and trained for the weighty responsibility of converting God's Word into their mother tongue. (A fifth, Reverend Joshua Arreak would be added to the team some years later.) It was a historic undertaking as it marked the first Canadian translation of the whole Bible that would be completed entirely by native speakers rather than missionaries.

The new, igloo-shaped Cathedral was an appropriate choice of venue for the 2012 celebration. As both the parish church for Nunavut's capital city Iqaluit, and the seat of the Diocese of the Arctic, it could be considered symbolic of the many Inuk churches and homes across the Eastern Arctic that had collectively given so much to make the Inuktitut Bible possible.

Because sacrifices were made along the way.

"The parishes did not suffer," says Canon Jonas Allooloo, now dean of the Cathedral and one of the original four translators. "We were parish priests and we had people working with us in the church," he explains.

But the men's families did.

Allooloo was a young, unmarried man when he started the translation work. Over the course of the next 34 years, he would marry, work fulltime as a parish priest and part-time as a translator, and together with his wife raise four children.

The project necessitated leaving families and churches behind for up to six weeks, twice each year, while the translators travelled south to work together or traversed the Arctic to research Eskimo dialects, unhampered by the demands of family and parish life. "We left our families to fend for themselves a lot," Allooloo says. "Sometimes children became rebellious. Some of us had to go home. Sometimes there was death in the family. Sometimes hospitalization."

But the priests were determined to complete the task they believed God had entrusted to them, recognizing that the Inuktitut Bible would ultimately prove to be a valuable gift.

The work itself was not easy. "Many living languages have no words to describe daily life in ancient Palestine," explains Hart Wiens, Director of Scripture Translation for the Canadian Bible Society (CBS). "For example, the Inuit people recognize six or seven seasons that do not really correspond either to English terms (spring, summer, fall, winter) or to biblical seasons (rainy, dry)."

Before missionaries introduced a written form of the language in the 1800s, Inuktitut had been an oral language for thousands of years. In the mid-twentieth century, as Inuit started to move into trading posts and the government established residential schools, English became increasingly common.

> THE WORD OF GOD IS A FOUNDATION OF OUR FAITH. IT CAN SUPPORT US AND IT CAN INSPIRE AND STRENGTHEN US.

The translators knew that having the ability to read Scripture in their own mother tongue would not only strengthen the people's faith, it would help to strengthen the language—and the Inuit culture—as well.

"The development of an indigenous theology needs indigenous language," says Mark MacDonald, National Indigenous Bishop for the Anglican Church of Canada in a CBS video. "So all over the world, but particularly here in Canada, we're realizing that even when people are fluent—especially when people are fluent in English—it's critical for the spiritual well-being of those people to be able to use Scriptures in their own language."

According to Statistics Canada, Inuktitut today is one of the most-spoken Aboriginal languages in Canada. It is the only indigenous language given recognition and status as an official language of a Canadian territory, Nunavut. Fully 68 percent of Inuit report it as their mother tongue. More than 36,000 people converse in the language and most of them are Christians. Indeed, in 2001—the last year for which data is available—more than 93 percent of Nunavummiut declared themselves to be Christians.

Upon completion of the project, the coordinator of the translation team and retired Anglican Bishop of Nunavik, Benjamin Arreak, expressed his hope that one day every Inuit home would have a copy of the Inuktitut Bible. "The Word of God is a foundation of our faith," he said. "It can support us and it can inspire and strengthen us."

Rebekah Williams is a lay reader at St. Jude's. She says being able to read the Bible in her mother tongue has made Scripture become "more alive. I can read it and I don't always have to refer back to English," she explains. "It was [translated] by people who were Inuit, who were thinking in Inuktitut as they translated. It's really wonderful to have that book from Genesis to Revelation. It's a real gift to Inuit."

Language is ever-changing, and Allooloo says for the Bible to truly remain in the language of the people, the work of translating Scripture must be ongoing. "A lot of our translations are still in the thinking stage," he says, noting that there are discussions around the possibility of creating a reference Bible, a study Bible, a Bible dictionary and more.

Like many mainline churches in the south, Allooloo says both his English congregation and his Inuit one skew older than the general population. No doubt that helps to explain why the new Bible is proving especially popular with older Inuit. Fortunately, Allooloo's current translation project is designed with younger generations in mind—with the support of the Canadian Bible Society, he's hard at work on a children's Bible.

ST. JUDE'S ANGLICAN CATHEDRAL
Iqaluit, NU | Ph. 867.979.5595
www.arcticnet.org/~igloocathedral

MORE TO EXPLORE

 Through a partnership with a non-denominational Christian charitable organization (the Canadian Bible Society) the Anglican Church of Canada was able to tap into the expertise and resources necessary to tackle a need in a community they never would have been able to meet on their own.

 According to the 2011 Census, almost 213,500 people reported an Aboriginal mother tongue and nearly 213,400 people reported speaking an Aboriginal language most often or regularly at home. Over 60 Aboriginal languages were reported. Despite the diversity of Aboriginal languages in Canada, three of them (the Cree languages, Inuktitut and Ojibway) accounted for almost two-thirds of the population using an Aboriginal language as mother tongue. **www12.statcan.gc.ca**

 Religiosity in Canada is lowest among young people. Clark, Warren and Grant Schellenberg. *"Who's Religious?"* Canadian Social Trends, Summer 2006, No. 81. **www.publications.gc.ca**

REFUGEE RELIEF IN SASKATOON

7. REFUGEE RELIEF IN SASKATOON

In the early 1990s, most of Bhutan's ethnic Nepali minority fled or were deported from their homes because of brutal new citizenship laws that discriminated against them. Amnesty International calls the resulting and ongoing situation in the South Asian country "one of the most protracted and neglected refugee crises in the world." Stripped of their nationality, more than 100,000 refugees settled in eastern Nepal.

Romesh Tamang, 30, was one of them. He was eight years old when he entered his first camp.

"I spent 20 years in the refugee camps," Tamang explains. On June 29, 2011, he arrived in Canada, the country he chose from the eight nations actively attempting to resettle the refugees trapped in the camps for so many years. Tamang is one of 6500 Bhutanese refugees that Canada plans to welcome as part of a global resettlement strategy.

Tamang settled in Saskatoon, Saskatchewan. Rick Guenther is one of the first Canadians he met, offering him both a Canadian friend and a Canadian church. Guenther is on the pastoral team at Meadowgreen House for All Nations, a church plant in a southwest Saskatoon neighbourhood with an immigrant population estimated at 80 percent. The church, occupying three bays of a strip mall at Avenue W and 18th Street, began as an outreach to immigrants by Ebenezer Baptist Church.

When Meadowgreen decided to offer a church service for the growing Nepali immigrant community in Saskatoon, Tamang, proficient in English and already a devout Christian after his conversion in the refugee camp, was the natural choice to lead it. The Nepali service is still firmly part of the multi-ethnic family of Meadowgreen, even though it is held in its own time slot with its own language.

"We talk too fast," explains Guenther. "We were losing them as far as the teaching goes. When they were in Nepal in the refugee camps, the Christians were getting together and someone with a little knowledge would get up and do some teaching. That has carried on here."

This partnership of mission, space and service is one of the distinguishing traits of the church. "From the beginning we've tried to partner with other agencies in town and that continues," explains Guenther. "When we first came in there we asked, 'who is doing what and how can we come alongside them and aid them in doing what they are doing?'"

There is Global Gathering, a service to immigrants that offers English classes at Meadowgreen four days a week. There is the Open Door Society that host conversation circles and presents cross-cultural awareness seminars in the revamped strip mall location as well. Mennonite Central Committee uses the space for a youth gathering. Local nursing students set up an outreach headquarters at the church twice a year for an eight-week nutrition and basic health skills blitz they offer in the neighbourhood as part of their training.

Kim Thiessen is the director of that program, and a nursing professor. She also attends Ebenezer Baptist. "It's an incredible opportunity for nursing students, an opportunity where I felt I could live out my faith in the context of my work life. God has called us to meet the needs of people on a very practical level."

Thiessen points out that she was not an expert on immigrant health at first but felt a pull that connecting fourth-year nursing students with new Canadians was an area in which she could possibly serve. "New Canadians come and have very specific health needs and often find it very difficult to navigate the health care system in Canada. People may experience decreased levels of health over a time because of that." The nursing students learn to be comfortable with a multitude of cultures, coming alongside and advocating for the needs of newcomers. "Often we have the fear of the unknown. Here we build a relationship and respond to the health needs in that context. That is the big win," says Thiessen.

> YOU'VE GOT TO BE SEEN AS A CHURCH THAT SERVES THE COMMUNITY AND NOT JUST BE THERE ON A SUNDAY GIVING SPIRITUAL TRUTHS AND HOPING PEOPLE WILL WALK THROUGH THE DOOR

"You've got to be seen as a church that serves the community and not just be there on a Sunday giving spiritual truths and hoping people will walk through the door," says Guenther. "You've got to get out there and serve whether they come to church or not."

When it comes to Canada's swelling immigration profile, Guenther says the message from the Church should be clear: "We are here for you and your family. We want to do what we can to assist you. We've given people driving lessons, given them rides, taken them to bank appointments, just practical stuff when they first come. We use the Bible to teach English. We have a conversation group specifically for Burmese people." The church opens up their facilities for free for African dance groups, Pakistani dance groups, weddings and funerals. "All kinds of people ask us if they can come and have a family gathering. If it's not being used we say, 'have at it.' We only charge if it's ongoing," says Guenther. "It's an attitude of serving the community."

And building community at the same time. Even as he understands why the Nepali community needs their own service right now, Guenther hopes it won't be forever. "You have to allow people of different ethnic groups to share and speak in their own heart language. When it comes to spiritual truths, when they get in their own group, all of a sudden it becomes clear," he says. "Ideally we'd love to see them be a part of us all the time. In the Book of Acts you see people of different languages and cultures gathering together."

Romesh Tamang is now surrounded by family, his own and his church family. He and his wife have two daughters, including one born in Canada. His parents, brother and sister arrived last year. He works at a recycling plant. "I'm glad I chose Canada," Tamang says. He has an easy answer when asked how Canadian churches can most effectively reach out to new Canadians: "Say hello. If they are Christians, invite them to church."

> "The practical one-to-one support the church gives makes all the difference. We find that when refugees live with us [at Matthew House] there is a sense of a caring community and a high trust level and openness develops because they see that we 'practically' care. But they are very reluctant to darken the door of a church unless someone has personally come to them and reached out where they are—showing that they genuinely care about them."
>
> – **Anne Woolger**,
> Founder and Director, Matthew House, Toronto.

MEADOWGREEN HOUSE FOR ALL NATIONS
501 Avenue W South, Saskatoon, SK | Ph. 306.249.0515
www.ebenezerbaptist.ca

MORE TO EXPLORE

 Kim Thiessen's experience offering her professional skills to create a nursing outreach to Saskatoon's refugees is a reminder that churches are filled with skilled visionaries often just looking for an opportunity to serve.

 The Canadian Council for Refugees is a national non-profit organization committed to the rights and protection of refugees and other vulnerable migrants in Canada and around the world, and to the settlement of refugees and immigrants in Canada. Their site lists resources and helpful links for congregations or individuals wanting to help. **www.crcweb.ca**

 Visit the Refugee Highway Partnership for tools and resources to equip the Church to most effectively serve refugees. **www.refugeehighway.net**

 Learn about Canada's refugee policies and how you can be involved at **www.cic.gc.ca/ refugees**.

OTTAWA, ONTARIO

CULTIVATING COMPASSION
— CREATING KOINONIA

8. CULTIVATING COMPASSION— CREATING KOINONIA

Many youth pastors ponder how they might cultivate compassion in their young charges. Jeremy Sauvé took his pondering one step further: as a youth pastor at St. Paul's Presbyterian Church in Ottawa, Ontario, Sauvé made a study of it.

As part of his work toward a Master of Global Leadership (with an emphasis in family, youth and culture) at Fuller Theological Seminary, Sauvé tackled the problem of cyber-bullying and the Church's response in an academic paper. Sauve grew to understand that a significant part of the problem that allows cyber-bullying to persist in our culture is the "bystander effect," that is, when young people see bullying taking place but choose either to join in or to do nothing.

Sauvé concluded that the way to tackle the problem was to create empathy. "One person willing to bring about a change can have a powerful impact because courage is contagious," he wrote. A seed of an idea blossomed into Sauvé's determination to inspire the youth at St. Paul's that they could each become "that one person."

Rugged and athletic, with a full beard that's starting to show some grey, Sauvé looks the part of a man comfortable with courage. He began to search out opportunities for the youth at St. Paul's Epicentre Student Ministry to cultivate empathy for their fellow human beings. In partnership with two consultants in the community, Sauvé developed Koinonia (Greek for "community"), a monthly drop-in social group for children and youth diagnosed with Autism Spectrum Disorder.

"Young people with autism, and others with disabilities, are prime targets for bullying," Sauvé explains. "It's my hope that by bringing the two groups together, our kids will learn to see autism in a new light, and to have empathy for these kids who struggle with enormous challenges."

He believes that the empathy birthed through Koinonia will overflow, influencing the young people's schools and online activity.

*

The atmosphere is electric when Koinonia meets at St. Paul's one Friday each month. Twelve to 15 teen volunteers from the youth group, together with four adult overseers, arrive first, at 5:30 p.m., for a volunteer briefing. Sauvé leads the briefing, which includes a short devotional and a time of prayer. Forty-five minutes later, the group gathers with an equal number of children and youth with autism from the community. Everyone arrives laden with potluck offerings, from sushi to popcorn, salads to casseroles.

The church youth mix with the community kids during dinner and for the social time that follows, featuring large group social games, or instruction in activities like martial arts or art therapy. Then the young people break into small groups for board and video games. At 9 p.m., the kids with autism go home, and the church youth linger for another half-hour to debrief.

"It took some time for both sides to get comfortable," says Sauvé, "but once that happened the excitement on both sides was palpable."

It's clear from watching the youth interact that genuine friendships are forming. The kids on the autism spectrum are gaining valuable practice in exercising social skills. Sauvé tells of a therapist who visited the program towards the end of its first season. "It took her a while to distinguish the youth with autism from the volunteers," he remembers.

Kerrie Kirkwood is a behaviour consultant (she runs a number of therapy programs for the autism community in Ottawa) and co-director of Koinonia. "These are kids who have grown up being the outsiders," she says of those on the autism spectrum, "knowing that they're different." But she's watching them thrive at St. Paul's, where they come eagerly each month, knowing they won't be bullied or judged. "The level of confidence they're developing is amazing."

> THESE ARE KIDS THAT HAVE GROWN UP BEING THE OUTSIDERS, KNOWING THAT THEY'RE DIFFERENT... THE LEVEL OF CONFIDENCE THEY'RE DEVELOPING IS AMAZING.

John Anderson serves as program coordinator and co-director with Kirkwood. In his day job, he teaches social and life skills to teens and young adults on the autism spectrum. "The average kid on the spectrum is running out of programs to go to," he says. "Most [treatment programs] available are for kids 12 and under. But socially, they're not that good on their own. Koinonia gives these kids a peer group of typical teens to interact with. And their social skills have improved dramatically. This program is giving them friendships."

Twelve-year-old Simon has rosy cheeks and a winsome smile. He sensed early that Koinonia was a special place to be. Following his first time ever at the group, he shared, "There are no bullies here."

"In my mind that's success," says Sauvé, "the beginning of a loving, accepting community reflecting God's love for the world."

But it's not only the kids with autism who value their new-found friends. Christine Desgroseilliers, 18, tells of a boy she met during the first year at Koinonia, named Leonid. "The first day, we just clicked. We had great conversations. At the end of the year, they told me he'd never opened up to anyone like that before.

"Being able to be a friend—I just loved that."

*

There is no spiritual component to Koinonia once the youth with autism arrive. "Our goal is to share the love of God, but not in the old-school, street-corner way," says Sauvé.

People must be sensing that love, however; one of the youth with autism has started attending St. Paul's regular youth program.

Anderson, who describes himself as an agnostic, was initially skeptical about partnering with a church. Today, he observes that the volunteer youth are "such an open-hearted, kind group of students." Then, speaking personally, he says, "It's a good experience for me to be at this church. It gives me a better connection with God as well."

> "Empathy, once learned and modelled to students unlocks the art of compassion in the students' lives. Empathy once unlocked can become a natural part of who they are as students and in return change the world that they are a part of."
>
> **– Matt Wilks**,
> Team Leader, Canadian Youth Worker

ST. PAUL'S PRESBYTERIAN CHURCH
971 Woodroffe Avenue, Ottawa, ON | Ph. 613.729.3384
www.stpaulspcottawa.com

MORE TO EXPLORE

 It's easy for youth ministry to become internally focused, seeking only to attract young people and educate them in Christian doctrine. But youth also need opportunities to flex their faith muscles by putting their faith into action. Koinonia gives youth both a chance to provide an essential service to an underserved demographic in their home community, and an atmosphere where they can learn how to empathize and care for those affected by a significant disability.

 Social media use is prevalent among today's youth. The biggest gains in use of social media are among young people 18 to 24 years old. Ladurantaye, Steve. "Canada tops globe in Internet usage." *The Globe and Mail*, March 1, 2012. **www.theglobeandmail.com**

 The second-highest social media users are the 18-and-under demographic. 'Individual Internet Use and E-Commerce', 2012. **www.statcan.gc.ca**

 Cyberbullying is any bullying "...that takes place using electronic technology ... such as cell phones, computers, and tablets as well as communication tools including social media sites, text messages, chat, and websites." **www.stopbullying.gov**

LACOMBE,
ALBERTA

ENGAGING HANDS AND
HEARTS IN COMMUNITY

9. ENGAGING HANDS AND HEARTS IN COMMUNITY

The city of Lacombe is nestled in one of Alberta's most fertile valleys between Calgary and Edmonton. It is at its roots a farming community, producing an abundance of local fruits and vegetables, livestock and animal feeds. This smallish city (population not quite 13,000) is a nice place to live—and for more reasons than its big central Alberta sky. The people here haven't forgotten their pioneering, homesteading, hard-work-and-community-building roots.

That is the spirit that infuses the congregation of Wolf Creek Community Church (WCCC), which started as a plant in 2004, and where Pastor Leon Johnston estimates "conservatively" that one out of every two congregants is involved in some sort of active volunteer ministry. They are "salt-of-the-earth" types, in the truest sense of Matthew 5:13.

"This church decided a few things early on that have probably helped in that process [of enlisting volunteers]," Johnston says. "If people want to become members, we invite them to sign a covenant that asks them to join us in ministry. So I think that has something to do with how things have played out here."

For a time, the church leadership considered abandoning the formal covenant. "It scares some people away," Johnston says, but on the other hand it also "keeps us accountable."

Johnston says the founding group led the way to creating this congregational buy-in to active ministry by actively engaging in ministry themselves. And they established a clear purpose statement: "Wolf Creek Community Church exists to reach out and enfold people to Jesus, together becoming devoted disciples of Him."

For a small church, WCCC works hard at pursuing that purpose. It takes helpers. Lots of them.

Hands and Feet Sundays require the most hands on deck. These two annual service Sundays (one in the spring and another in the fall) are how the church is best known in the community.

The day begins with a short worship service before people leave the building in teams, dressed to work. Margaret Devries, deacon and founding member, says this year they'll have 13 teams of various sizes involving upwards of 60 percent of the congregation. She rhymes off some of the projects they'll tackle as a way of expressing care for their community: highway clean-up, visiting a seniors' lodge and leading a worship time there, gardening and yard work for seniors and disabled people, building a wheelchair ramp and re-shingling a garden shed for a disabled couple, helping another disabled woman with housework, building maintenance for the local pregnancy care centre and other ministries.

"We also plant potatoes for the food bank," she says. "We plant them in the spring and harvest them in the fall. This year, we're going to have 5000 pounds."

The church works hard at motivating people to be involved. Devries observes that, "We all have the same amount of time. What's necessary is to help people to see that serving in the church is an important thing to do. And it's a fun thing to do."

Matching the right people with the right projects, she says, is also critical.

Janis Butcher has been co-leading WCCC's other key outreach, Mom Time, for four years. Chat with her for a few min-

SHIFTING STATS

> WE ALL HAVE THE SAME AMOUNT OF TIME. WHAT'S NECESSARY IS TO HELP PEOPLE TO SEE THAT SERVING IN THE CHURCH IS AN IMPORTANT THING TO DO. AND IT'S A FUN THING TO DO.

utes and her passion for this ministry makes it clear she's the right person for the job. Some 80 women and 60 children register for this weekly Thursday morning Bible Study and mentoring program that offers good food, conversation, prayer, crafts for the kids and special guest speakers to inspire the moms. It takes 27 volunteers each week to keep the program running smoothly, and it's part of Butcher's job to find them.

"I got up one Sunday morning and stood before the congregation and said, 'Help!'" she says. "[Volunteering] is just a small bit of our time, and maybe we feel like 'it's insignificant and what difference does it really make?' But it's not our time. It's God's time. We're doing God's work. When He has workers, He can do amazing things."

Jodie Spurrell is in her second year of coming to Mom Time with her two preschoolers. "It's been a blessing in my life," she says quietly. "I had just moved to Lacombe. I didn't have any friends or family here. And I was desperately needing to find a place to meet other moms."

Spurrell says the volunteers who make the program possible provide an "invaluable" service. Knowing her children are well cared for and happy allows her to relax and enjoy the weekly break. "It's been very healing for me," she says. "This is a place of acceptance. And the Bible studies have helped me on a personal level."

Butcher concedes she didn't really know what she was getting herself into when she said yes to co-leading Mom Time. "It sounded like a good idea to me, so I said 'Sure.' And then God said, 'Now I'm going to change your life.'

"I have no leadership training or background," Butcher adds. "But God said, 'I'm going to use you.'"

Seeing how God has used her own willingness to serve inspires her to invite others to volunteer. "Seeing what God can do in my life is huge motivation," she says, "because He can do it in their lives, too."

> "I believe that churches can paint a clearer picture around what it means to be part of the 'body of Christ.' It's also important to help church members address the root drivers behind busyness and consumerism while also not driving them into relentless church activity nor using the lures of consumerism to keep them in our pews."
>
> **– Steve Brown**, President, Arrow Leadership

WOLF CREEK COMMUNITY CHURCH
4110 Wolf Creek Drive, Lacombe, AB | Ph. 403.782.4563
www.wolfcreekchurch.ca

SHIFTING STATS

MORE TO EXPLORE

 At Wolf Creek Community Church, the leadership laid the foundation for an active, engaged congregation by establishing a strong statement of purpose, setting the example of serving in ministry themselves, and by inviting members to sign a membership covenant asking them to join in the church's ministry.

 A lack of time is the biggest barrier to people becoming involved in volunteering. About two-thirds of Canadians ages 15 and over who did not volunteer in 2010 said the key reason was not having enough time. Vezina, Mireille and Susan Crompton. "Volunteering in Canada." *Canadian Social Trends*, Component of Statistics Canada Catalogue no. 11-008-X, April 16, 2012. **www.statcan.gc.ca**

 By asking congregants to commit to volunteering for short-term projects like Hands and Feet Sundays, church leadership has been able to engage a high percentage of volunteers.

RENOVATED ROOMS
—AND RESTORED LIVES

10. RENOVATED ROOMS—AND RESTORED LIVES

The story goes that sometime around the year 1212, an 18-year-old woman named Clare ducked out of her family home in Assisi, Italy and ran off to become a follower of an up-and-coming, destined-for-fame preacher named Francis. Francis welcomed her, disguised her and squirrelled her away in a convent where she was protected from her father's repeated attempts to abduct her and marry her off so she could have children.

Instead, Saint Clare of Assisi—or Chiara in Italian—founded The Order of Poor Ladies and dedicated her life to the service of those in need. Her inspiration lives on in a unique, hard-won housing project engineered by a little Canadian church that could.

As the crow files, Assisi is 7634 kilometers away from downtown Winnipeg. Chiara House, named in Clare's honour, just opened at 490 Maryland Street in Winnipeg's West End, 802 years after Clare ran off.

Chiara House is an apartment building with three floors and a full basement. Each floor has three suites: a two-bedroom, a one-bedroom and a bachelor. The newly renovated rooms are filling with the conversation and activity of their first residents.

One-third of those who will live here live with mental health challenges—and will often be people in the process of transitioning to greater independence from some kind of care program. One-third of those who move in will seek out Chiara House because they need affordable housing in a gentrifying neighbourhood where real estate prices have rocketed 361 percent in value in recent years. The final third who will call Chiara House home will do so very intentionally and prayerfully, out of the missional mindset nourished by their home church, Little Flowers Community. The lines blur, with some residents fitting into one, two or all three groups.

"Early on as a church we found we were drawing people who would not always fit or feel comfortable in a typical church setting, including people with mental illness," says Jamie Arpin-Ricci, Little Flowers' pastor and an urban missionary with Youth With a Mission Urban Ministries Winnipeg. One of those people was a young man who lived—and then died tragically—with a severe, untreated mental illness. Arpin-Ricci was there the day his friend jumped off the roof of a University of Winnipeg building.

Arpin-Ricci remembers walking down the street to his home, surrounded by fellow church members. "For the next three days, half of our church moved into our house so we could be together and care for people." There was comfort in community. And time to think about what could have helped their friend.

"We recognized the need to provide stable and secure community for people living with mental illness," says Arpin-Ricci. "We recognized how critical housing was to that process. People would go from in-patient treatment to their own apartment or room. It was too big of a step. We needed to create space for people to have housing and independence, but to be surrounded by people who could support them."

Then something wonderful happened. An innocent question was posed to Arpin-Ricci (one with which every church planter everywhere is familiar): When is your church going to have a building?

His answer: "If we were going to have a building, we would make it an apartment for people living with mental illness."

Arpin-Ricci is an avid blogger, so in 2010 he wrote about his growing vision for supportive housing for people living with mental illness. "A friend in the Mennonite world shared it with some Christian business people. They said, 'We want you to have the freedom to do what you do well, and not be burdened.'"

The business people offered to buy, renovate and manage an apartment building for Little Flowers to use for this ministry. "They allowed this tiny church to expand our capacity and it gave Christian business people a chance to do more than write a cheque," says Arpin-Ricci. The partnership expanded to include Mennonite Church Manitoba, which provided support and funding, and Eden Health Services, which offers mental health support when needed. "It's a great partnership that sees different organizations, that might otherwise do things separately, come together."

> THEY ALLOWED THIS TINY CHURCH TO EXPAND OUR CAPACITY AND IT GAVE CHRISTIAN BUSINESS PEOPLE A CHANCE TO DO MORE THAN WRITE A CHEQUE.

It has not been easy. The renovations involved a lengthy three-year journey with volunteers and all the normal setbacks and complications. Youth groups showed up to paint. Retired tradespeople gave months of their time. There were spirit-busting break-ins and vandalism. Tools were stolen. There were fires. Three of them. Deadlines were discarded. But in the fall of 2014, Chiara House was finally ready.

The end result is more than just housing. It is community. The bachelor suite on the main floor is designated as a community-gathering place. Donated board games and paperbacks fill the shelves of a bookcase. One wall is painted a brilliant orange—a signature colour of Little Flowers. The kitchen will bring forth casseroles and pot roasts, meals to share from time to time so everyone is reminded they are not alone.

This is the Church being the Church to a segment of Canada's population that is notoriously underserved and often left out in the cold, literally. Families of loved ones living with mental illness can be dramatically affected by their loved ones' struggles as well, as they attempt to care for and protect their family member. "As we understand more and more about mental illness, and understand the significant numbers of Canadians who live with varying degrees of mental illness, we believe there is a role for the Church to come alongside and offer help, like community and friendship," says Arpin-Ricci. "This helps the individuals and it also helps the families who can be overwhelmed and at a loss."

Jon Owen and his wife Joelle Kidd have moved in to Chiara House. They are the caretakers of the building and members of Little Flowers. They will also be caregivers and of course, care-receivers as they dive into the reality of this unique community. "It makes sense to me that we would be involved in each other's lives in a more tangible way," says Jon Owen. "When you look at the idea of living intentionally together, it's acknowledging those intersections with each other's lives, it's acknowledging we need each other. There's another layer that says I'm a part of something bigger, I am part of a community of people who depend on me and could benefit from my involvement in their lives. That is contrary to a lot of individual impulses in society."

Where society tends to exclude, Chiara is built to include. "For people who have mental health illness, there is a lot of disclusion from society. The idea of creating community and including those who have been disclused is important to me," says Owen. "We've all been disclused at some point."

LITTLE FLOWERS COMMUNITY
443 Furby Street, Winnipeg, MB | Ph. 204.898.7319
www.littleflowers.ca

SHIFTING STATS

MORE TO EXPLORE

 The Church, says Arpin-Ricci, needs to begin to address and destigmatize mental illness. "We often spiritualize these issues and put people at greater risk. We need to educate ourselves about mental illness, to know when we don't have the capacity to help someone. That's why we partner with Eden Health Services."

 According to the Canadian Mental Health Association, a stable and supported living environment is "essential to maintaining the health and well-being of people with serious mental illness and is integral to their recovery." Enhanced life skills, better health and an "increased sense of empowerment and involvement in the community" are all results of a stable living environment. **www.cmha.ca**

 Chiara House also includes an emergency suite and laundry facilities built to share. Residents can offer hospitality to others in need.

LOWER SACKVILLE, NOVA SCOTIA

A PODCAST CAN
CHANGE YOUR WORLD

11. A PODCAST CAN CHANGE YOUR WORLD

They had her at the podcast. When Jamie Lynn Wilkinson, 26, a Halifax-based university student, saw signs around the city for Shiloh University Church, she was intrigued enough to find it through Google.

Her search led to Twitter, Facebook, and almost immediately to a podcast of a recent worship service designed especially for her demographic. She listened. She liked. And then she emailed Mike Miller, student pastor at Rock Church in Lower Sackville, Nova Scotia, the church behind Shiloh Uni, as it is affectionately known.

"I explained my story, that I was looking for a new church, just trying to figure out how to start a relationship with God," says Wilkinson. Miller connected her with another young woman who attended Jamie's school and was on the Shiloh Uni leadership team. They met. They clicked. And Jamie began attending the Friday night service usually held in a rented room on the Dalhousie University campus.

Halifax is a student's city. There are six universities and numerous colleges that bring in students from across the country and around the world. More than 25,000 undergraduate students alone call Halifax home from September to May each year. Jamie's story cannot be unique among them. She went to church as a child, but wandered away from her faith when she left home for school. She partied with the best of them. With a downtown core jammed with bars and pubs and within walking distance of at least a few of the major campuses, Halifax's nightlife booms and beckons. "I drank a lot," says Jamie. "That is the culture in the world right now. But it wasn't me. Deep down I knew there was something more out there."

At Shiloh Uni Church, she found her tribe. Although she couldn't have known it the day she searched for the church, Jamie's story fit perfectly with the mission of this service. A driving force behind "why we started Shiloh Uni was our realization that some of our own kids were deserting church at 20 and during the first year of college," explains Russ Conway, lead pastor of Rock Church. "We have to be able to have an answer to this."

Shiloh Uni is church brought directly to campus for kids who might otherwise check out when they hit campus—if they ever attended at all. There is a full band. The music is loud and long. And the preaching does not mince words or skimp on the altar call offered each and every week. A team of 40 young adults helps set up, plugging in lights, setting up a guest services station, checking the sound.

Students stop to listen during the service and some wander in each week, astonished that the band rocking the room has anything to do with church. "Because the music is good and people are their age, it's such a shock to people," says Jamie. "I've had someone say to me outside: 'Wow, you guys are Christians. They come in all shapes and sizes,'" she recalls. "They didn't even know there were young people out there who loved God. It's so funny to me."

They do, however, "know from the time they come that it is church," says Miller. "If we leave the message strong, they continually respond. Shiloh is a biblical name, but it can sound like a fraternity. It may have hurt us in the short term, but we wanted people to walk in and expect the Bible, hymns and God, and I think we surprise them by speaking their language."

After the service, usually about 80 of the on-average 200 attendees head downtown to a coffee shop to visit and enjoy each other's company. "Over coffee and gelato seem to be where relationships start," says Miller.

> WE WANTED PEOPLE TO WALK IN AND EXPECT THE BIBLE, HYMNS AND GOD, AND I THINK WE SURPRISE THEM BY SPEAKING THEIR LANGUAGE.

Even though the Rock team is thrilled that students are coming out on Friday night, they don't want to send the message that students have a hall pass from Sunday morning. "We try to encourage them not to look on Friday as their church, but to see it as dessert," says Conway. Because only on Sunday morning does the essential dynamic of multi-generational community come to life. "Being multi-generational is so important—seeing strong examples of marriage, singles at retirement age, that strong generational connection when so many other things are polarizing. We want a community that is all ages." In fact, when Conway teaches a Church 101 class—an introduction to Rock Church for those who may be newcomers—two-thirds of the attendees these days come from Shiloh Uni.

As for Jamie, "I have found my church family," she says. Her friendship with the young woman Pastor Mike connected her with after listening to the podcast has bloomed. "She and I have been best friends since that day. You have a different kind of bond with people who believe the same thing as you."

Recently, Jamie spent three and a half months in Cambodia for her Honours thesis, researching the care offered to victims of sex trafficking after they have been rescued. She listened to Shiloh Uni podcasts the whole time she was away.

A PODCAST CAN CHANGE YOUR WORLD

"Today's youth want to change the world. Social media and other technologies give them the capacity to have outsized and immediate impacts. Knowing this lowers their patience with structures that force them to wait to be involved until they're 'adults.' If they can't plug in at church, they will somewhere else and by the time we're ready for them they'll be otherwise occupied."

– **Rick Hiemstra**,
Head of Research for the Evangelical Fellowship of Canada,
co-author of *Hemorrhaging Faith*

ROCK CHURCH
222 Sackville Drive, Lower Sackville, NS | Ph. 902.864.3553
www.rockchurch.ca

MORE TO EXPLORE

 From Sunday service to Sunday School to Shiloh Uni, Rock Church podcasts it, taking advantage of the digital revolution to bring the Gospel message to as wide an audience as possible.

 If you can speak a sermon into your iPhone, you can do a podcast, say Russ Conway and Mike Miller at Rock Church.

 "We as a church believe the message cannot change but the medium can. There has never been a more digitally connected age than right now," says Conway. "Youth and young adults are so transient. They go off across the country and around the world. They want to stay connected."

IMMIGRANTS: WELCOME TO THE ISLAND

12. IMMIGRANTS: WELCOME TO THE ISLAND

Joy (Sangkee) Park speaks a precise but cautious English. He searches his ever-expanding vocabulary for the correct word to describe just how hard it's been, in fact, to learn this complicated language with its more than 900,000 words, its inconsistent vowels and its auxiliary verbs that turn sentences into rough terrain for new English speakers.

"I am 46. For Korea and China, most of the Asian countries when I was a student in high school or university, speaking English was not important for us," explains Park.

Now speaking English feels like one of the most important things of all. Park arrived in Charlottetown, Prince Edward Island in October 2012. Winter hit him like a freight train. So did the pressing need to learn the language so he could begin to build his new life. Park signed up for classes at an English language school but it was a friend who introduced him to the conversation group run by Cornerstone Baptist Church. Every Tuesday night, Park joined dozens of fellow immigrants to this Maritime city to practice conversational English with church volunteers happy to sit for an hour to talk.

"We tried to sit down and build relationships," says Gordon Dickinson, Cornerstone's pastor of community outreach. "We wanted them to feel welcome and comfortable with us, as simple and basic as their English was." Cornerstone itself is located in the suburbs, so the conversation circles take place in a downtown Salvation Army building.

"We probably wouldn't have anywhere the kind of ministry we have if we hadn't been willing to partner and do it in their building, even if that meant the people found their way to their church," says Dickinson. "Their captain [pastor] had arrived in the city at a similar time to me. They saw there were a lot of newcomers in the city. We told them we'd love to partner with them to do that work."

The question explored by the two churches was: "What can we do together?"

"How can we help?" was the other formative question, only Dickinson put this query to the PEI Association for Newcomers to Canada (PEI ANC), a nonprofit that provides short-term settlement services and long-term integration services for the growing numbers of new immigrants in PEI.

"I emailed them and said, 'My church would like to do something with newcomers. Could we meet and you can tell me what the needs are and what we could step into?'" recalls Dickinson. "The man who received my email was very supportive of churches wanting to engage with new Canadians in this way."

Joe Byrne was that man. As Community Connections Supervisor, he was happy to hear from a ready-made community of friendly Islanders who were willing to roll up their sleeves and volunteer. Volunteers were needed for those services that help newcomers survive—helping them settle, find shelter, and have other basic needs met—and for helping new immigrants thrive. "Many of those needs are relational," says Byrne. "When you engage with community [like a church] that pre-exists, you are engaging with people who are already in relationship who can engage, challenge and love each other."

Byrne says Dickinson is "our key conduit into the rest of the community. We can access with one phone call dozens of people because of the relationships that exist." That, says Byrne, makes it both a very attractive partnership and a very "efficient relationship. We can generate huge numbers of volunteer hours because of those relationships that exist and the nurturing behind it."

> OUR PROGRAMS ARE SECULAR. BUT OUR RELATIONSHIPS ARE SPIRITUAL.

Cornerstone proved their mettle the very first time they called PEI ANC, when Byrne asked for volunteers to help transform the downtown area known as the beautiful Victoria Row into the setting for their annual DiverseCity Multicultural Festival. The Cornerstone team did the "grunt work" of setting up dozens of tables, chairs, garbage cans and picnic tables. And then they put them all away again 11 hours later. "It showed we were willing to participate and help," says Dickinson. "They also said they were always looking for people to partner one-on-one with newcomers to develop their English skills. We could see there was a need for English support."

That's when the English conversation group formed. Cornerstone hasn't stopped there. Together with the Salvation Army, they threw a Thanksgiving Dinner with all the fixings, something that has become an annual event. "We had 40 from the church involved. We worked from 9 to 6. We cooked turkeys, decorated the tables. We had all our waiters and waitresses dressed in black and white," says Dickinson. "We did the best possible dinner we could do."

It's all about welcoming immigrants into relationship while meeting felt needs. The goal is not to proselytize: "Our programs are secular," says Dickinson. "But our relationships are spiritual. Our ministry has been based around the ideas of hospitality. That was the approach Jesus had," he says. Friendships form during English practice or at special events like the Thanksgiving Dinner. Those relationships usually grow to include the extended family of immigrants. "From there, you just suddenly meet somebody and you run into them on the street, or go and visit to say hi, and all of a sudden you meet eight family members."

Dickinson brings his work home quite regularly—and dramatically. Last Christmas, he and his wife briefly worried whether their floor would collapse when 50 people from the English conversation group came over for a party. At Easter, there were 65. "An Asian man sitting on my couch looked around," says Dickinson "and he said, 'everyone at Gordon's house is happy.' He couldn't get over that."

Cornerstone is creating a kind-of-but-not-really church service now, for newcomer friends who want to learn more about Jesus and explore Christianity.

"The biggest need was English, but there have been all kinds of other things, like helping people with food, groceries, beds. I don't know how many times I've helped people move. We see a real interest in spiritual things," says Dickinson. The problem, though, is the level of English used in most church services is just too high and too quickly spoken for most immigrants trying to learn the language.

The weekly worship experience Cornerstone is creating will include storytelling using simple English and worship songs. "It will include more of a Bible study than a sermon. We will have small discussion groups. I don't know if I'm even comfortable calling it a worship service, because people aren't necessarily coming to worship. We're calling it Mosaic." Cornerstone thinks of this service as something like a youth group: "a specific demographic within the church that we hope won't be disconnected forever, but who need their own special place for a time."

And if the idea needs tweaking, they will fix it on the fly. Dickinson has been part of ministries before where everything is planned out in advance—or that was the attempt. "With this, I've seen such a dynamic of not knowing what God will do, even in an instant. For this work, we have had to be willing to set aside our own ambitions and plans and be willing to go where the Spirit leads. We have no idea what we are doing most of the time."

As for Joy Park, he had some serious homesickness but now, he says, he is better. "My English is okay. I have some friends in PEI. It's better than before."

> "Jesus said to his disciples, 'Look around you, the harvest is ready.' We continually need to be reminded of 'the invisible' around us."
>
> – **Dan Sheffield**, Director, Global and Intercultural Ministries, The Free Methodist Church in Canada

CORNERSTONE BAPTIST CHURCH
9 Cornerstone Drive, Charlottetown, PE | Ph. 902.892.1001
www.cornerstonebaptist.ca

MORE TO EXPLORE

 In 2014 PEI ANC had more than 1152 registered clients.

 Gordon Dickinson says that members of Cornerstone have been changed by their interaction with newcomers, as much as the newcomers have been helped. He recalls one "dyed-in-the-wool Islander" who set aside her fear of those who were different and came to be a full, enthusiastic volunteer for the English conversation group.

 As part of his research for how to run a conversation circle, Dickinson visited a church in New Brunswick that ran a similar program. He came back with piles of material, but he simplified the material more and more with each passing week, providing basic conversation starters and topics to aid with the discussions that took place.

KEMPTVILLE, ONTARIO

COACHING AND CONNECTING TO TACKLE DEBT

13. COACHING AND CONNECTING TO TACKLE DEBT

The day Sarah* walked into the Kerith Debt Freedom Centre of North Grenville Community Church in Kemptville, Ontario, she carried a grocery bag stuffed with mail she was afraid to open.

Her small business in the pet industry was not doing as well as Sarah felt it should and could be. Her accounting books were a mess. Years of just getting by as a single mother had taught Sarah that the envelopes crashing into her mailbox were not stuffed with good news. Bills were bombs ready to detonate when opened, a visit to the bank a frantic dash through a battlefield.

"It was a cycle of ridiculousness," says Sarah now, a year after surrendering her bag of bills to the coaches of the Debt Freedom Centre.

That day, the volunteers Sarah would come to view as her team gently slit open each envelope and deactivated their charge. They stacked junk mail and bills into orderly piles.

"I felt like I wasn't alone," remembers Sarah. She left her appointment with an emptier bag and a lighter spirit. The groundwork was starting to be laid for a plan that included her returning every two weeks to work through her mail with her team, learning to question and eventually release an unskilled bookkeeper, and a plan that would, a year later, see Sarah finally and fully debt-free.

Debt was no stranger to Dan Massey either. He is lead pastor of North Grenville Community Church. And as an IT specialist turned pastor, Dan and his wife had to adjust their lifestyle to a new, lower salary level. They had found themselves in bondage to their debt, like thousands of other Canadians whose salary can't seem to catch up to their spending.

The Masseys had plodded their way out of their financial pit with the help of a Christian program, one they happily paid for. The seeds of appreciation were planted in them for a Christian-based debt relief program built on biblical principles.

But what if it was free? And offered through the church?

Enter the Canadian National Christian Foundation (CNCF) and their ministry arm, Advisors With Purpose, with an almost built-to-order model for churches. In fact, North Grenville was the pilot church for The Freedom Initiative.

"We wanted to help churches be the place where people turn to in need, and freedom from the bondage to debt was a desperate need in our churches and communities," says Jan Kupecz, executive director of CNCF. "We wanted to equip the Church to be the place that could offer real help and hope."

The vision is big: a national network of local churches empowered and trained to see people and families in their communities free from the burden of debt. Advisors with Purpose trains church volunteers and helps the local congregations establish Debt Freedom Centres. The centres provide free face-to-face debt advice to anyone in their community who needs it. Each centre is encouraged to connect with local community resources and professionals where they can refer clients as appropriate and when needed. The church pays CNCF a one-time fee for signing up and a small monthly amount to pay for ongoing training.

The coaches, explains Massey, "are everyday people from the congregation. They've been trained by CNCF. We also have greeters to help people assimilate into the environment. If you come, you may be nervous." Non-Christians especially may wonder what they are getting into, says Massey. Spirituality never comes up unless the person asks. The Centre is located at the church itself, and is open the second and fourth Saturday mornings of each month. "We are generally booked up," he says. The profile of people seeking out the service is diverse: "People who are on social assistance to people making six figures. Debt knows no boundaries."

Some visitors come in once, and that's all they want or need. "Others will come in and say 'I need to buy a car. Can you help me see if I'm in a position to get one?'"

Massey is clear on the terms: they offer coaching, not consulting. It's a relationship, not a program. "If they want to stay with us forever, they can."

Ultimately, for Massey, it's about the family. "It's about holding the family unit together. That's the economy of God, the household," Massey says. "It's getting people's money straightened up so they don't have the debt to pass on to their children, so they can save for their children's education. It's about quality of life."

Sarah's quality of life is on the upswing. "My phobia of mail and banks was like a phobia of spiders," she says. "We laugh about it now, and it still creeps up, but I have people in place to help me with that."

DEBT KNOWS NO BOUNDARIES.

The most profound lesson for Sarah was recognizing, "I do have control. Just as long as I realize it." She also sees this kind of community service offered by a church— her own church in this case—as a welcome development in how the Canadian Church helps people in financial need. All too often, she says, people show up at the church office to tap into benevolent funds. That can be necessary, for a time, but it doesn't get to the root of the issue. "The Church would rather be nice than assertive sometimes," says Sarah. Encouraging those same folks to visit a Debt Freedom Centre—even if it means carrying in plastic bags brimming with unopened mail—can be the step that, in the end, truly does set them free.

*Sarah is not her real name.

NORTH GRENVILLE COMMUNITY CHURCH
2659 Concession Road, Kemptville, ON | Ph. 613.258.4815
www.ngccfm.ca

MORE TO EXPLORE

 Advisors with Purpose offers a booklet: "Things to Consider Before Opening a Centre" that you can request online at **www.advisorswithpurpose.ca**

 The Canadian Financial Capability Survey that tracks Canadian debt defines household debt as mortgage debt and consumer debt: credit cards, lines of credit, bank loans and unpaid bills. *Household Debt In Canada.* **www.statcan.gc.ca**

 More than 60 percent of household debt in Canada is held by Canadians under 45 years of age, nearly half held by couples with children. *Household Debt In Canada.* **www.statcan.gc.ca**

REGINA, SASKATCHEWAN

ENGAGING YOUTH—
BUILDING RELATIONSHIPS

14. ENGAGING YOUTH — BUILDING RELATIONSHIPS

The night starts with just one ball hitting the hard gym floor of Cochrane High School on Froom Crescent in Regina, Saskatchewan. It is the distinctive, familiar *thunk, thunk, thunk* of rubber + wood + kid. The sound builds until it's a tropical rainstorm of balls as the gym fills with neighbourhood kids piling in for Align Youth, a sports night with a Gospel twist presented on Friday nights by The Compass Church.

Compass has its office in this neighbourhood with its boundaries easily defined by Froom Crescent, the street that wraps around and tucks in near the Trans-Canada and busy Arcola Avenue.

Align is about providing fun mixed with Gospel for the neighbourhood kids, the majority of them from lower-income immigrant families. It's also very much about launching Christian kids from Compass into ministry. "We stretch the Christian kids out of their comfort zones," says Murray Lutzer, Compass' youth pastor. Each Friday night, "We meet at a restaurant at 5:30 with the Christian kids and that's our discipleship time." Lutzer refers to research that shows once kids are out of high school "there is a huge disconnect with the Church, because they haven't been empowered. They've been babied."

Compass has paid a price for putting on a youth group that expects the Christian kids to show up and serve, instead of the more traditional template of games and teaching. "We've had people leave the church because we don't cater to that. We don't see other youth groups as wrong, but this is a vision God has put on our heart that is deep-seated," says Lutzer. Align even has its own catchy tagline: "Youth pastors to kids who would never have a youth pastor." As Lutzer says, "There is no age limit to missional living."

Align is also the garden out of which something new is growing for Compass Church. They're calling it Mission Regina. And if it had a clever tagline, it might be: Christian community for families who would never have Christian community.

The idea is simple. Compass adults will also start coming to Align, and befriend the kids. They will do things like walk kids home (with the parents' permission, of course) and go right up to the front door and shake hands with Mom and Dad. They will pop back for a visit. They might take the whole family out to dinner. They will do more listening than talking, trying to figure out the family's practical and spiritual needs and how Compass might help. How Compass might be a "hub of help," says Lutzer.

"A lot of the people we are working with are Muslim," he explains. "They are a long way from home and they have no family here. What really birthed Mission Regina was a desire to help the transition to Canada, especially in Regina." When he says especially in Regina, yes, Lutzer is talking about the winter. "For seven months we are all isolated in our houses. You can go a long time without seeing your neighbours. We're like: 'Let's go and impact these new families.'"

The Align team had tried to reach out to the families before, by inviting them to come to the gym night. That idea flopped like a deflated basketball. "No one would show up. They wouldn't come," says Lutzer. "We knew we needed to do something about this and be intentional about the families. We want to be able to help them out where their needs are. You can't really know someone if you're just guessing what their needs are. That [failed gym night] was what showed us that we don't have a relationship with the families."

> **THERE IS NO AGE LIMIT TO MISSIONAL LIVING.**

Lutzer is leading the way with his own family. He and his wife have taken a Somali family out to Dairy Queen for dinner. Five out of eight kids. The parents didn't come, but conversation and trust are building. "We made sure it was clear what we were doing so it wasn't as weird. They know us because we would go and pick up their kids in the winter," says Lutzer.

Jordon Fontaine and his wife Sam, Compass volunteers, have launched another Align night in a different Regina neighbourhood, this one predominantly First Nations. They have begun the process of making the double connection with the kids who come and the parents who send them. "Whether that is hanging out, going to a football game or just building into the family's lives. Right now we're just trying to build relationships with the parents," says Fontaine.

Compass has missional home groups as part of their congregational life. One of those groups has embraced the spirit of Mission Regina and is throwing around balls on a Friday night at Align, so they can begin to meet the families through the youth. Lutzer says, "They will be able to say, 'We want to get together with you. We want to know who you are. If there's something we can help you with, we'll help you.'"

THE COMPASS CHURCH
70 Froom Crescent, Regina, SK | Ph. 306.522.3685
www.compassregina.com

MORE TO EXPLORE

 When Compass Church shifted their focus to involving their own youth in active outreach, they lost some members of their church who didn't agree with the emphasis. They were willing to pay that price.

 The website **www.canadianimmigrant.ca** has an entire section devoted to the variable Canadian climate. Anyone interested in understanding the immigrant family experience of winter should check it out.

 80 percent of the families Compass Church reach out to are Muslim. The Canadian Network of Ministries to Muslims offers resources at **www.cnmm.ca**.

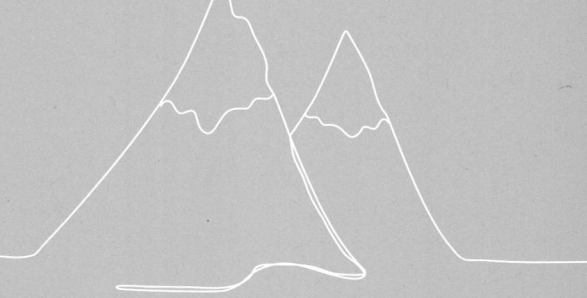

RICHMOND, BRITISH COLUMBIA

STRONG MARRIAGES, STRONG COMMUNITY

15. STRONG MARRIAGES, STRONG COMMUNITY

New Joy Church in Vancouver, BC, is not afraid to talk about sex, communication, how to have a good fight—and all those other things that go into making a marriage strong. Even from the pulpit. A major focus of this growing, multi-ethnic, multi-generational church in Richmond, British Columbia is ministering to families and marriages having a tough time sticking together in Canada's changing culture. The intimate life of a married couple is an essential ingredient in any successful relationship, so it sometimes gets talked about in sermons and especially in the Love After Marriage workshop, a 10-week focal point of the church's family ministry.

"In light of our world in which the sanctity of marriage is being diminished in our society, we don't want to be that church that speaks against something, but instead, the church that speaks for something," says Steve Kim, New Joy's senior pastor. New Joy offers extensive pre-marital counseling and a menu of marriage seminars. Bad and broken marriages repeat themselves through the generations, believes Kim, but so can good ones. "We focus on family and marriage because we want to leave a good model for generations to come."

The Love After Marriage (LAM) workshop is an American-made program, adapted by New Joy to fit their congregation.

What they especially like about LAM is its emphasis on vulnerability and communication—carried out within the context of Christian community.

In other words: expect to get to know the other couples sitting at your table very, very well.

Jimmy and Aeri, married for 19 years, realized pretty quickly when they went through LAM that no marriage was as perfect as they had thought. "We had no idea that other couples were going through similar things we were going through," says Aeri. They were already good friends with the couples who shared their table—they just hadn't shared the truth about the struggles in their marriages with each other. The sharing would continue after the DVD and discussion group ended, with the four couples intentionally meeting together to support each other in their ongoing work to improve their marriages.

Then one night, one of the couples had a fight in front of everyone else. The wife cried. "That broke the ice," says Aeri. "Then every meeting someone would bring up something. More often than not, the wife would break down in tears. And then it would get tense and awkward." The other couples would listen and then gently observe what they thought was happening. "Hearing it from a third party would neutralize the emotions a bit. It was from someone who loves us. Everyone is in the same boat," says Aeri. "That's been our journey. I feel like anytime I've had any huge leaps forward in my walk with God, it's been in community. We are real with each other."

Healing through being real is also the experience of Brian and Doris Ha, a married couple who are also New Joy's Family Ministry Pastors. As staff, they were required to go through LAM. "The culture in our church has changed in the last five or 10 years. As a church it's very normal now to talk about our sex lives openly with other couples." Brian acknowledges this openness is probably a surprise to new church members, especially if they haven't yet gone through LAM. "I'm certain it is uncomfortable at the beginning to talk about it. Our people share about their challenges and a lot of shame is worked off," says Brian. "You realize you're not the only couple struggling with it. We know it's probably one of the main sources of conflict for couples. To see people be really open about it, to be transparent and vulnerable, really helps the other people in the group to be very open."

There are two common wounds that the Christian community can use deep healing from, they say. One is the overwhelming prevalence of pornography. The other: the ugly tendrils of shame left over from wrong (even if rightly intended) Christian teaching on sex.

> WE SEE A LOT OF COUPLES WHO BRING IN THE IDEA THAT SEX IS WRONG OR BAD… [WE WANT THEM] TO SEE IT AS BEAUTIFUL AND DESIGNED BY GOD.

"We see a lot of couples who bring in the idea that sex is wrong or bad, and they carry those ideas into marriage," says Doris. "It's been so heavily engrained in them. That is one thing that we see in a lot of married couples. To get over those hurdles of porn and the mindset that sex is dirty. To see it as beautiful and designed by God. We focus the last third of the workshop on intimacy and what God's design for sex is in marriage."

It's been a great tool, says Steve Kim, for this church with such a focus on marriage and family. "It is very intensive. People are forced to talk about their marriage in front of others. They realize others are going through the same issues and that really helps them." There has been breakthrough after breakthrough, he says, including in his own marriage. He is not afraid to share his and his wife's own history of seeking marriage counseling and their ongoing work to keep their marriage healthy. "If the leaders are open, others will be open," he says. "And the more we are open, the more people tend to be open."

New Joy believes marriage is the "starting point for community," says Brian. "If you have strong marriages, you have strong families and strong individuals. When people are learning to love the other, and learning how to grow in conflict, you will really grow in community as well," he says. "Marriage is a microcosm. It is the mystery of Jesus and His Bride."

Marriage is also capable—in the day-in-and-day-out-ness of it all—of being a profound incubator of forgiveness and redemption, another reason it is worthy of so much tender loving care from New Joy Church.

NEW JOY CHURCH
11295 Mellis Drive, Richmond, BC | Ph. 778.789.5598
www.newjoychurch.com

MORE TO EXPLORE

 Encouraging couples to be vulnerable—with each other and in front of each other—is helping to build strong marriages at New Joy. Couples are building honest friendships that are genuinely helpful to each other's marriages.

 In John Freeman's book *The Tyranny of Email: The Four-Thousand Year Journey to Your Inbox* (Scribner, 2009), the author reports that 65 percent of Americans spend more time with their computer than their spouse.

 In The Good News About Marriage: Debunking Discouraging Myths About Marriage and Divorce (Multnomah, 2014), author Shaunti Feldhahn shares that Christians actually have a divorce rate up to 50 percent lower than the general population.

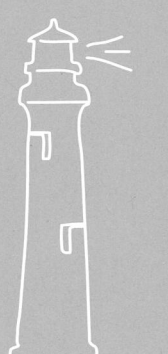

MONCTON,
NEW
BRUNSWICK

WATCHING VOLUNTEERS
FLY IN MONCTON

16. WATCHING VOLUNTEERS FLY IN MONCTON

James Carpenter was far outside of his comfort zone and not liking it one bit. When the 19-year-old stood in front of 200 people at his church's annual volunteer appreciation night, accepting the award for Volunteer of the Year, he just wanted the moment to end. "I'm a behind-the-scenes kind of person and they called me out on stage and all that," says James.

James received a camera bag and $200 to acknowledge his extra ordinary presence as a faithful volunteer at Moncton Wesleyan Church. "It's a good feeling to be recognized," concedes James. But, "I'd rather not be on the stage."

As the tech guy at his congregation, James is in high demand to record events and produce videos for his church, a congregation that averages 1300 on a given Sunday. He was also the creative eye behind a set of videos of volunteer testimonials created for another volunteer appreciation event, which was later shown by the church to recruit even more people into ministry within the congregation.

James is one of more than 400 volunteers in this congregation. "They are a lifeline. They are an extension of everything we do," explains Lil Harris, Director of Groups and Volunteers. "They work at it like a job if we do it the right way. It allows us to maximize our potential."

Lil believes volunteerism is probably underutilized in a lot of congregations, including their own. "To get people engaged as volunteers, you have to be intentional about inviting them into ministry," she says. "The approach has to be that we are helping them use their God-given gifts in a field of the church."

That's exactly how James feels. He's one of those digital guys who grew up in front of a computer, seeing what was possible. "I really like the technology aspect of it, I find it enjoyable," says James. "I'd rather be doing something than not; it's a bonus that you're building the church and helping. It's a really good feeling. If you can work at an event for a lot of hours, you come out of it feeling good." Because he makes things look so good, and probably so easy, James is in high demand. At a certain point, in fact, his youth pastor recognized that everyone and their dog was calling James wanting his help.

"I guess you could say I got overused," laughs James. "The youth pastor asked them to go through him—that way I didn't have to say no to them. I could say no to him. I'm a little more on my own now because he left. I have learned to say no to some things."

Care of volunteers like James is high on the list of priorities for Lil. "When I took over this role four years ago, my natural bent was to encourage volunteers...to be a champion of volunteers." That means making sure volunteers aren't victims of multiple, competing demands from different departments, and that they are thanked well and often.

Clarity is also essential: of the role, duties and expectations that go along with each position. Lil is developing job descriptions, "whether it's a greeter or a preschool worker. It makes the person accountable and brings clarity to what the ask is. For instance, if you want to be a greeter, you have to be at church 15 minutes prior to the service. You create expectations that are mutually agreed upon. It gets you on the same page.

"It is absolutely important," adds Lil, "that volunteers feel they are part of the mission, so we have their buy-in and support, so they can be an ambassador for the mission of the church.

People can get burned out very quickly if they don't realize how valuable they are."

Encouragement, says Lil, is a biblical principle. "I believe so highly in the importance of encouragement. It's a lifeline for people to stay involved in ministry."

> YOU HAVE TO BE INTENTIONAL ABOUT INVITING THEM INTO MINISTRY...HELPING THEM USE THEIR GOD-GIVEN GIFTS...

Gifts are another biblical principle, and helping people discover their giftedness—so they can then work in that zone—is another essential element of managing volunteers with busy lifestyles. "People sometimes don't know themselves what their passion is or what they are good at," says Lil. Other times, Lil has had church members volunteer for positions that surprised her. "Sometimes, volunteers can self-appoint. I need to give more credibility if they determine where they can fit. Conversely, sometimes people come to you, and if you get to know them as an individual you can speak into their lives and say, 'I think you'd be good at this because of how I see you.'" They may flop, says Lil, or they may soar like an eagle.

When volunteers do fly, the church is freed to live out its mission more fully in the community in which they find themselves. "You can't do enough of that," says Lil. "That's where the Body of Christ needs to be."

"This church is intentional about its volunteers: enabling gift discernment, matching the gifts to the tasks, providing clarity about assigned tasks, expecting accountability, being attentive to potential burnout and providing meaningful recognition. Above all, this church has in place a person of high skill and intuition who ensures that volunteers are cared for and will journey with them. A superb model for other churches."

– **Suzanne Lawson**,
Coordinator, Together in Mission,
volunteer expert Anglican Church of Canada

MONCTON WESLEYAN CHURCH
945 St. George Boulevard, Moncton, NB | Ph. 506.857.2293
www.monctonwesleyan.com

MORE TO EXPLORE

 It was James Carpenter's youth minister who recognized that James was being over-used and having a difficult time saying no to multiple requests. He created a structure to protect his young volunteer.

 Volunteer Canada offers a Canadian Code for Volunteer Involvement to support organizations that engage volunteers and help them evaluate their current volunteer engagement program. **www.volunteer.ca**

 Charity Village offers an online course in "Building a Great Volunteer Program," available at **www.charityvillage.com/elearning**.

 The Anglican Church of Canada offers a free online course, "Engaging Volunteers in Ministry: A Deeper View of Stewardship." Find it at **www.anglican.ca/gifts/ministry-webinars**.

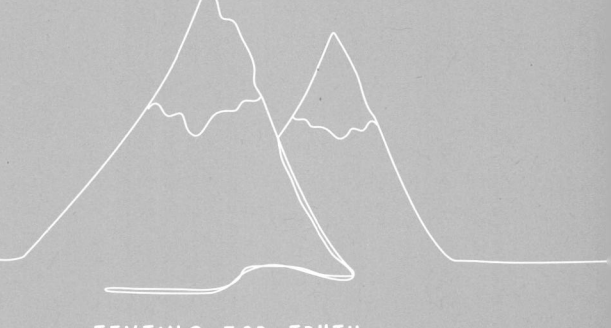

TEXTING FOR TRUTH

17. TEXTING FOR TRUTH

When an underground electrical fire and explosion caused a power outage in the west end of Calgary, Alberta on Thanksgiving weekend 2014, the folks at Kensington Commons Church, just outside of the affected area, knew intuitively what would be among the community's most urgent practical needs. On the morning after the outage, they posted the following invitation to the church's Facebook page: "For those without power this morning: if you were planning to come to church anyway we can get you some breakfast and get your mobile devices charged up for you."

The offer of a free device charge also went out to a much broader audience via Twitter. "We figured we'd invite anyone who was stranded without power," explains Jeremy Duncan, lead pastor at Kensington Commons. "People were looking for charging stations, and that's just what we offered them." But, he adds, "We didn't want to give people the impression that we were bribing people to come to church."

Duncan's not sure how many non-church people came through their doors to take advantage of the free power. He guesses there were a few in the morning and a few more that evening. Nobody was counting. It was the gesture itself that had meaning, for it was "generally indicative of how we're trying to interact with the community," he says. "We want to be open and accessible to people."

It also demonstrated that Duncan and his ministry team know their people—and their neighbours—and that mobile computing devices are a critical part of those people's lives.

Like much of the neighbourhood in which it is located, Kensington Commons Church is composed largely of young, urban professionals. These are well-educated ones, with good careers and the salaries to go with them. They've grown up using technology, and they're not only comfortable with the latest high-tech toys, they're dependent on them.

In his mid-30s, Duncan is himself a member of that young adult generation.

Slight of build, with long brown, centre-parted hair and beard, he looks a little like those Sunday School portraits of Jesus. "The main driving piece in our community is probably intellectual engagement with faith," Duncan says. "So we go at things from a fairly intellectual bias in terms of how we engage. The downside of that is that people may not be engaged emotionally or in terms of patterns and traditions connected to their faith journey."

To address that reality, Kensington Commons incorporates elements of liturgical worship in their otherwise contemporary Sunday morning services, like the invitation or call to worship, reading a weekly psalm from the lectionary, prayers of confession and response.

Sometimes, the response takes the form of the Eucharist or a liturgical reading. Sometimes it is a time of silent reflection. And sometimes, it comes with a contemporary twist, one that acknowledges today's technology trends. During Duncan's teaching time, the congregation is invited to send in their questions via text message. Then, following the sermon, Duncan answers some of those questions—or takes questions from the floor. They call it "Q & R" (question and response). It is a deliberate strategy to stimulate engagement.

"Part of doing Q & R is to reinforce to our community through liturgy and pattern that the voices that matter aren't only the voices that come from the front of the room with microphones," he explains. "Responses come from all of us."

Congregants can text a question every week, at any time during the service if they so choose, but Q&R happens only once a month or so.

Mike Sharp, 22, has texted questions during the service. "It's a really easy way to be able to get out some thoughts that you have during the message," he explains. "You can't interrupt when someone is speaking, but if you have this question that you really want to hold onto, you can send it in [via a text message] right away."

Duncan isn't able to respond to every question during the service, of course. For questions that must go unanswered due to time limitations, "He'll get back to you during the week," says Sharp.

Frequently, Duncan's answers lead to longer conversations that become telephone chats or meetings over coffee. "Usually I just respond by text," he explains. "Sometimes it's a fairly easy answer. Sometimes it's more complex. Then what I'll do is say, 'Hey, listen. Text is a hard way to answer a complex question—so here's a quick answer. If you want to grab a coffee, let me know.'"

"I have two days a week that are booked to meet with people and talk with people about their questions," he says.

Kensington Commons has embraced technology in more ways than just texting in questions during the service. They have an active social media presence, a YouTube channel and do regu-

> PART OF DOING Q&R IS TO REINFORCE TO OUR COMMUNITY...THAT THE VOICES THAT MATTER AREN'T ONLY THE VOICES THAT COME FROM THE FRONT OF THE ROOM WITH MICROPHONES.

lar podcasts for those in the community who might miss a service. They don't take up an offering during the service: most of the congregation's 400 people give online or through automatic contributions, although there is a box in the lobby for those few who want to contribute cash or cheques.

The church also publishes a journal—in both print and digital formats—that maps out an entire 52-week calendar, outlining the teaching for the coming year, with space for people to journal their notes. Duncan explains that journaling can be a helpful way for people to hear and "digest" ideas; the act of writing thoughts down or typing them into a smartphone or tablet helps to solidify new insights.

Ryan Quist, 32, uses both the digital and print journals. "I'm an IT guy," he says. "Technology is just part of the way I interact with the world. But I use the [print version] too."

Intriguingly, far more people in the congregation have embraced the old-fashioned method of taking notes. Jenna Tyson, 28, explains that she finds journaling with pen-in-hand to be, somehow, "more kinesthetic, more present." She says she tries to avoid digital devices altogether at church because she finds being online can be distracting. "I end up on bunny trails, because you wind up checking your texts or whatever."

Being open and accessible to people at Kensington Commons Church clearly means embracing new technology and its users alongside older traditions and practices.

KENSINGTON COMMONS CHURCH
2404 Kensington Road NW, Calgary, AB | Ph. 403.283.0654
www.commonschurch.org

SHIFTING STATS

MORE TO EXPLORE

 More than one in five households in Canada have cell phones as their only form of telephone service. In 2013, 21 percent of households reported using a cell phone exclusively, up from 13 percent in 2010. Exclusive cell phone use is more pronounced in young households where all of the members are under 35 years of age. In 2013, 60% of these households reported using a cell phone exclusively, up from 39% in 2010 and 26% in 2008. Statistics Canada, *Residential Telephone Service Survey 2014*. **www.statcan.gc.ca**

 Canadians sent a total of 96.5 billion person-to-person text messages in 2012, representing a 23.7% increase over the 2011 total of 78 billion messages. Canadian Wireless Telecommunications Association: **www.txt.ca**

 Churches that support online giving report increases in giving by their congregations. **www.businesscloudnews.com**

WHITEHORSE, YUKON

MAKING ROOM IN
CANADA'S NORTH

18. MAKING ROOM IN CANADA'S NORTH

Not a single soul.

That's who Joy Allen knew when she landed in Whitehorse, Yukon, after an 11,500 kilometre flight from Singapore.

Allen disembarked from the plane—a mere 700 kilometres south of the Arctic Circle—into the snowy world she had glimpsed from the windows as the craft descended. Moving from the part of the world where she was born and raised in the Philippines marked a leap of faith into the wild unknown. She left behind family, culture, familiar food and activities, all for a shot at a better life. Allen would be only the second nanny from the Philippines ever to work in Whitehorse.

Robert Young is a transplant to Whitehorse, too. He is associate pastor at Bethany Church in this city he is so passionate about. Young moved here from parts south and wouldn't consider going back. "Like most people, I just fell in love with the community and ended up not leaving," says Young.

And what's not to love? Wilderness City, as it's known, is wrapped in mountains and edged by the mighty Yukon River. The economy is healthy and the air is clean. Whitehorse made it to *MoneySense Magazine*'s top places to live in Canada list, ranking first for cities with fewer than 25,000 people in 2011.

All that Whitehorse has to offer is not lost on the growing Filipino community. The word diaspora is not misused here. Filipinos are attracted to Canada's North for the wages, healthy and high compared to back home where the average annual salary hovers at around $2500 USD. The Yukon Nominee Program promotes immigration to Canada's North, streamlining the process for foreign workers happy for the opportunity.

Bethany Church found itself ministering in a changing city.

If you walk down the road, says Young, "and see different ethnicities, your church should look the same. We are open to wherever God is leading the church. We are open to whoever He brings to our door."

God eventually brought Joy Allen to Bethany—Young calls her "the godmother of this group." The group is the Filipino congregation who meet at Bethany, a part of the church but just a little apart still, preferring to worship in their own language to feel that connection with home and God once a week.

The presence of the Filipino congregation and culture in Bethany has changed the church for the better, says Young. "It brings a richness, it brings a family together. God's family has different ethnicities—why wouldn't we in the four walls of the church as well?" he asks. "It's been a good challenge for us to be able to stretch ourselves to make room for the people God is bringing to our church. It means not being so limited, so focused on one people group."

This melding into the Church usually happens one by one. One recent arrival to Whitehorse meets someone just slightly more settled who invites them to church. That's how it was for Allen. Church provided a way to meet people and find her place in the community.

"If you are lonely, you can just cling to somebody," says Allen. "Church is where I find my solace, a place I can go to that is caring, loving. They provided for me, too. They invited me to their homes. It is a home away from home."

Church, says Allen, is like a magnet for her and for the other Filipinos she knows in Whitehorse. "You can speak your own language and feel more at home. You can sing songs in your language. It brings you back home."

And, if you connect with Bethany Church, you can pack your bag for Camp Yukon, a church-run camp on the shores of Atlin Lake. It offers all the joys of camp, including chapel, swimming, canoeing, kayaking, crafts, and even riflery and paintball.

The Filipino contingent at Bethany have their own special time at Camp Yukon. The kitchen rolls out dishes like tinapa (dried fish), roasted pig, and sticky, delicious bilo bilo rice. A Filipino speaker completes the weekend's offering. If a weekly service provides community and comfort, the annual retreat at Camp Yukon super-charges that impact, creating memories and bonds that sustain the group throughout the year.

> CHURCH IS WHERE I FIND MY SOLACE, A PLACE I CAN GO TO THAT IS CARING, LOVING. THEY PROVIDED FOR ME, TOO. THEY INVITED ME TO THEIR HOMES. IT IS A HOME AWAY FROM HOME.

"I'm so thankful to our church and the other churches here that have opened up their doors to the Filipino community," says Allen. "They have really opened their doors, not only to build my relationship with the Lord but to know that you can still have family in the church. You feel included." Allen's experience of the Church responding to the immigrant population in Whitehorse has been defined by approachability and welcome. "It's wonderful to have the Church being sensitive to the immigrants." And Allen, the woman who had never played in the snow, eventually learned how to ski.

Robert Young remembers a time when he was a youth pastor

ministering in the high school. He would go eat lunch with students and saw that there was a table for the Filipino students and a table for white Canadians. "In a few years I have noticed those tables are gone," says Young. "I believe in the Church, it will be the same way." The two services at his church, he feels, will merge into one. He won't put a timeline on it. But he believes it is coming.

BETHANY CHURCH
91806 Alaska Highway, Whitehorse, YT | Ph. 867.668.4877
www.bethanychurch.ca

MORE TO EXPLORE

 www.canadianimmigrant.ca is an excellent website to understand Canada from the immigrant's experience and viewpoint.

 World Vision Canada, with partners Tyndale Intercultural Ministries Centre, published a report entitled: "Beyond the Welcome: Churches Responding to the Immigrant Reality in Canada" that includes trends as well as suggestions and tools for Canadian congregations. **www.communitybasedresearch.ca**

 In 2012, Canada broke its own record for welcoming newcomers, with 257,515 newcomers crossing Canada's borders. **www.canadianimmigrant.ca**

HALIFAX, NOVA SCOTIA

RESHAPING TRADITION
— REVITALIZING YOUTH

19. RESHAPING TRADITION — REVITALIZING YOUTH

Have you heard the one about the bats in the belfry?

It's one of those Christian jokes that pop up on clean humour websites and serve as mildly funny and all-too-true lines in sermons by ministers in mainline churches. A church can't get rid of the bats in the belfry. Then the youth pastor confirms them... and they're never seen or heard from again.

Saint Benedict Parish in Halifax, Nova Scotia will never tell that joke. Bats in their clean, modern, well-lit interior are highly unlikely. Plus, the culture in this Roman Catholic Church has changed dramatically—especially in terms of how they minister to and with the youth that make up a growing segment of their church body.

Confirmation is a sacrament in the Roman Catholic world. The traditional faith journey of a young person begins with infant baptism, then First Communion, and then typically a few years later (usually around grade 9) culminates in confirmation. At confirmation, the teenager owns the faith that was expressed at baptism on the infant's behalf, and their initiation into the Catholic Church is complete.

Then, all too often, like bats liberated from the highest arches of a cathedral, the teens disappear from church life. It's as if they have graduated from something, not into something.

Father James Mallon is parish pastor of Saint Benedict. He's the author of *Divine Renovation: From a Maintenance to a Missional Parish* (Novalis, 2014) and he serves on the board of Alpha Canada. Mallon is proud that the number of young people being confirmed in their parish is down and their conversion rate is up. Not as many kids are being confirmed, but those who are really mean it.

"We are making our programs not informational, but transformational," says Mallon. "We want them to have an experience of Jesus and the Holy Spirit. Then they become teachable."

The parish tossed the classroom model of teaching out the stained glass window four years ago, and ushered in a "youth group model." They unhitched confirmation from any particular age. "Confirmation happens when you are ready," says Mallon. "People can be ready at all different ages. It's a question of helping them be prepared."

Parents who haven't heard about the change still call up to report their child is now in grade nine and ready to be confirmed—even though they haven't been to church since their First Communion. "It's become a ritualized apostasy," says Mallon. "Confirmation is a sacrament of communion. They see it as a sacrament that releases them from the life of the church. Our integrity is at stake."

Youth Alpha is playing a big role in this church's transition to a disciple-making model of youth ministry. It is a Canadian-made version of the popular evangelism-through-discussion series— but crafted especially for young people. The video clips are provocative, engaging, and occasionally funny. They deal with questions like 'Who is Jesus? And what exactly does he want from us?'

Ronnie Lunn is Coordinator of Youth Ministries at Saint Benedict. He says, "Youth Alpha is the best tool I know" for what the church is trying to do with their youth. Everyone who comes to the church's junior high program goes through Youth Alpha. "It is baseline evangelism," says Lunn. The 12-week program provides the youth with what Lunn calls "a common language." He adds, "It's not preachy. They will feel accepted. We are challenging teens to engage with their faith and their culture."

> **WE ARE CALLED NOT TO CHANGE THE CONTENT, BUT WE ARE CALLED TO COMMUNICATE THAT TRUTH TO A CHANGING CULTURE.**

Where traditionally a focus in a youth gathering may have been on catechesis (what we believe and why), Saint Benedict's focus is on evangelism. "Our big philosophy," says Lunn, "is that everybody coming to a youth night will receive a message that will speak to them, that is relative to them. They won't have stuff go over their head. We engage the culture and the problems teens are facing both in and outside the church."

This involves the kids who come to church and those who don't. "We are reaching out to those who aren't in the Church, which is the mission of the whole Church, which we have forgotten and are rediscovering," says Lunn. "It's the Great Commission, it's the final thing Jesus says to do in the Gospel. For a long time it hasn't been 'go'—it's been stay in the church and do what you do."

On Monday nights, Saint Benedict is crowded and loud. It's youth night for grades six through 12. If you missed it, or if you are a curious parent, you can listen to the weekly podcast posted on the church's website. Youth night at Saint Benedict is appropriately called The Experience. That's at the heart of what they are trying to do: have youth experience the living faith of a relationship with Jesus Christ.

"Oppose by all means the status quo mentality, those crippling words whispered and shouted in churches: 'That's the way we do things here,'" says Mallon. "The Gospel is unchanging. We are called not to change the content, but we are called to communicate that truth to a changing culture."

SAINT BENEDICT PARISH
45 Radcliffe Drive, Halifax, NS | Ph. 902.443.0725
www.saintbenedict.ca

MORE TO EXPLORE

 Saint Benedict moved from a "ministry as usual" model to a new way of doing things, and they have not looked back.

 Youth Alpha is available at **www.alphacanada.org**

 Roman Catholics in Canada account for half of all Canadian Christians. *History of the Church in Canada.* **www.cccb.ca**

20. PURGE SUNDAYS: INNIES AND OUTIES

Walk into the worship warehouse that is the home of The Meeting House (TMH) in Oakville, Ontario at 8, 9:30 or 11:15 on a Sunday morning, and you could be forgiven for thinking you had stumbled into a rock concert rather than a Sunday morning service.

Illuminated by pink and purple lights overhead, row upon row of theatre-style seating fills as hundreds of people, many carrying coffee cups, choose their places. A five-piece band plays loud, chest-thumping music from the stage. Manned video cameras throughout the room point toward the musicians, while large screens on either side of the auditorium display branded messaging.

It is September, a time when church attendance across the country typically swells with the return of congregants who've been away throughout the summer months. For The Meeting House, that means it's a good time to ask people to consider making a demonstrable commitment to TMH—or to leave.

As congregations go, The Meeting House is one of the largest of the large. More than 5000 people regularly gather at 18 Ontario locations of this multi-site church each Sunday morning.

So it might come as a surprise to learn that The Meeting House regularly invites people who don't want to get plugged in to get out.

Known to church staff by the tongue-in-cheek label of "Purge Sundays," the invitation to "get in or get out" was the idea of teaching pastor Bruxy Cavey, as a way of addressing the reality of Christian consumerism—and the thousands of people who come through the doors of The Meeting House each year in the course of "shopping around" for a church that best meets their needs.

"We would like to challenge people," Cavey explains, "that if for some reason you don't feel that this is a good church for you to serve at, then go find a church where you can."

And people listen. Both attendance and donations have historically taken a dip within a week or two of Purge Sunday. But at the same time, volunteer numbers surge.

Purges happen once or twice each year. This time, they're occurring in the context of what's being called "Frosh Kick-Off," a three-week series that sees the leadership dressed in sky-blue T-shirts emblazoned with large "TMH" letters, and Cavey looking almost collegiate in a burgundy V-neck sweater with the block letters, "TMHU."

The teaching time this week is titled, "Surviving and Thriving at TMHU." Cavey walks through the biblical basis of what normative Christian life in community looks like. The first week focuses on what it means to be a disciple, the second will examine what it means to serve, while week three addresses mentoring and the need to commit to a "house church" or small group.

As the series progresses, Cavey drops increasingly less subtle hints that people need to get with The Meeting House program. "It would be sad," he says, "if people were just to come to TMH as consumers, and if we were to be okay with that."

Life is busy, he concedes. Time is tight—for all of us. That's why TMH has intentionally moved to a model that restricts mid-week programming, asking people instead to commit to active participation—in the form of Bible study, relationship building and serving—in a house church.

> IF FOR SOME REASON YOU DON'T FEEL THAT THIS IS A GOOD CHURCH FOR YOU TO SERVE AT, THEN GO FIND A CHURCH WHERE YOU CAN.

"We are a network of house churches that also has a Sunday service program on the side," he explains. He says if people cite busyness or lack of time as factors for limiting participation, they are encouraged to commit to house church, and forego the Sunday gathering, because it is in genuine community where real discipleship takes place. "You can't make home church an add-on," he says.

Being a passive, Sunday morning observer is discouraged. If someone is spiritually seeking, or uncertain about whether they want to follow Jesus, then they are invited to sit back and listen, but they're still encouraged to actively participate in asking their questions and learning. It tends to be longtime believers, or people who've become accustomed to church culture in other contexts, who struggle most with the notion that they're being invited to leave.

"We'll have people come up afterwards and say, 'If you keep talking like that, I just might not show up,'" Cavey says with a chuckle. "And we'll say, 'Well, that's the point. We really believe this.'"

> "Can you imagine having parts of your own body that are disconnected or not working? Since a core image of the Church is the 'Body of Christ,' we can assume that all members are to be connected and actively engaged for the Body to function biblically and effectively."
>
> – **Steve Brown**,
> President, Arrow Leadership

THE MEETING HOUSE
2700 Bristol Circle, Oakville, ON | Ph. 905.287.7000
www.themeetinghouse.com

MORE TO EXPLORE

At The Meeting House, leaders are not afraid to demonstrate they value people's time by encouraging those who have not yet made a commitment to their church to either do so or to find another church to which they would be comfortable making such a commitment.

Time stress is a reality for many Canadians. In 2010, 34 percent of people aged 15 and over reported feeling trapped in a daily routine. The proportion of people who took part in social activities declined from 66 percent in 1998 to 59 percent in 2010. People spent less time socializing with friends and relatives, including face-to-face and telephone conversations and restaurant meals. *General Social Survey- 2010 Overview of the Time Use of Canadians.* **www.statcan.gc.ca**

The busyness of contemporary life is taking a toll on many churches. Sunday mornings have become a catch-up day for many Canadians, who use the time for family activities or chores that they didn't have time to complete during the week. Shifting the emphasis away from Sunday morning worship to an alternate day—or even to mid-week small groups—can help to keep people engaged who might not attend a traditional Sunday service.

CHARLOTTETOWN, PRINCE EDWARD ISLAND

EMPOWERING KIDS AND
STRENGTHENING FAMILIES

21. EMPOWERING KIDS AND STRENGTHENING FAMILIES

Emma stood in front of the congregation of Calvary Church in Charlottetown, Prince Edward Island holding three clay pots as the object lesson of her sermon.

One pot was broken in shards, another was smooth and perfect. The third pot was shattered but had been pieced back together. The preacher shone a light through it to show God's ability to redeem the broken. One man was so moved, he wept in the pews.

Emma, the preacher, is 10. She is part of a young and growing team of children and youth in this Island church who lead worship, pray, receive the offering, disciple others, travel on and off the Island to visit other churches to lead worship and yes, preach with the best of them.

It's not that Pastor Phil Taylor's pulpit has been taken over by a youth uprising. It's simply that this Pentecostal Assemblies of Canada congregation fiercely believes that there is no such thing as a "child-sized anointing of the Holy Spirit." Whatever an adult can do in church, a kid probably can too. "Children will respond to opportunities to be disciples of Christ at an early age," says Taylor. "They experience Christ. They understand." And they want to be released into ministry in the Church. "One of the most exciting things you'll ever see is the moment when these children are leading adults to Christ, whole families are getting the information and taking the Bible and sharing their faith," says Taylor.

All this happens through a program (which is more like a movement) called King's Castle. It is this church's answer to families adrift; parents have to agree to fully support and participate in the training and empowerment of their kids. It is also an answer to the marginalization of kids into cute kid story moments and parallel programs that may make young people feel they really do have to wait until tomorrow to be the Church.

And, yes, it's old-fashioned, Pentecostal-style evangelism. But "it's also about keeping families together, and making a strong family," says Taylor. In the three years the church has used King's Castle they have seen families grow closer, and watched the confidence and leadership muscle of youth grow stronger and stronger. "There's nowhere in the Bible where it says there is an age to be released into ministry," says Kimberly Murray, Calvary's Children and Family Life pastor.

"Hearing myself talk about it, I realize it really is an incredible role reversal," says Taylor.

It is a role reversal in more ways than one. Unlike the traditional trajectory of programs and resources travelling from the West to countries around the world, King's Castle is an import—straight from El Salvador.

The church discovered King's Castle during a mission trip to that country, where the curriculum is known as Castillo del Rey, a youth evangelism and empowerment movement Taylor calls "an army of light." Spread throughout most of Latin America, Castillo del Rey takes teams of youth into the roughest of neighbourhoods to preach the Gospel and engage in social justice projects.

"We were so impressed with this, and when we came back to Canada we realized we have nothing here like this. Our curriculum is about consumption and not development," says Taylor. "It's an adult world in church." Calvary set out to translate the curriculum from Spanish to English and to transform adult

> **THERE'S NOWHERE IN THE BIBLE WHERE IT SAYS THERE IS AN AGE TO BE RELEASED INTO MINISTRY.**

church to everybody's church. They are the only church in Canada using the program.

"We're receiving this from El Salvador—we've learned from them," says Murray. "I think sometimes in the West, we have this idea that we've got the goods and the rest of the world needs to learn from us. This is a great example of how we need to learn from developing countries. They have things to teach us. We had to import this because we didn't have it."

She adds, "We wanted to move children from being entertainment and cute to having their own spiritually anointed ministry and taking the lead in the church. They preach. They lead. That's what we saw in El Salvador. And we wanted it here."

> "Churches should be constantly trying to reduce the lag time between teaching and application. Youth prefer experiential learning, and reinforcing biblical teaching by doing is one of the ways youth validate what they hear."
>
> **– Rick Hiemstra**, Head of Research for the Evangelical Fellowship of Canada, co-author of *Hemorrhaging Faith*

CALVARY CHURCH
9 Capital Drive, Charlottetown, PE | Ph. 902.368.1226
www.calvarycharlottetown.com

SHIFTING STATS

MORE TO EXPLORE

Giving children more responsibility at church did not push kids away from attending; the effect was quite the opposite. Kids are clearly capable of more than we think. That's what Calvary is discovering.

Visit Castillo del Rey at **www.kingscastle.org**

The report "Hemorrhaging Faith: Why and When Canadian Young Adults are Leaving, Staying and Returning to Church" discovered that youth feel more attached to a church where they are released into ministry, and when their contributions are valued and respected. **www.tgcfcanada.org/hemorrhagingfaith**

GATINEAU,
QUEBEC

ALL IN THE FAMILY

22. ALL IN THE FAMILY

When Peace Nyiraneza lost her husband to a brain tumour in 2006, her world shattered. Left with the daunting task of rearing their four children (then ranging in ages from three to 13) alone in Rwanda, she decided a fresh start was what they all needed. And she decided Canada was the place to get it.

"I had heard a lot about Canada," she says. "About the education for the children and so on. And so I thought, 'By God's grace, maybe He will open the doors.'"

He did. It took just over two years to work through the immigration process, but together the family arrived in Canada in 2009, settling in Gatineau, Quebec. "I didn't want to go to a big city like Toronto or Montreal," Nyiraneza explains, "and get lost there with the children."

Besides, she is a woman of deep faith and she believed Gatineau was where the family was meant to be. "When I have to make a big decision I sometimes ask God to give me a sign. Sometimes I get a sign that shows me the right way," she explains. Two different friends had talked to Nyiraneza about Gatineau, suggesting the smallish city would be a good place for the family to locate. It was all the confirmation she needed.

It wasn't long before the family met their new neighbours; one couple in particular seemed especially kind, and took a genuine interest in helping the family. When Nyiraneza learned they were Christians, and members of Église chrétienne du Plateau, she decided, "That's the church for me."

But Nyiraneza didn't have a vehicle. "So they organized rides to church for myself and my children. Five of us," Nyiraneza says, a note of wonder in her voice. "For the whole year! It took two families—all year long—to drive us all."

Nyiraneza says the first time she walked through the church's doors she felt at home. She connected immediately with another recent African immigrant—a woman from Burundi. The two would become best friends.

But the help that church members provided extended beyond rides and friendships. They offered guidance in navigating the countless unfamiliar Canadian systems that newcomers must learn. The church offered excellent programs for children and youth that allowed Nyiraneza to feel supported and not quite so alone: scouting and leadership training for her son; Vacation Bible School for her younger children in the summer; Christmas gifts during the holidays.

"When I came to this church, I understood what I have been hearing since I was a child," says Nyiraneza. "That the Church is a family. The whole week I would be at home, running around, dealing with the schools, and such things. I would really feel like I was in a foreign country. But when I'd get to church on Sunday, I felt like I was among family. I was home."

*

Quebec's fourth largest city, Gatineau is also one of the province's most rapidly growing municipalities, thanks to immigrants like Nyiraneza: close to 10 percent of the population was born in a country other than Canada.

It is not surprising that newcomers should be attracted here. Gatineau is prosperous. Its proximity to Ottawa means an abundance of public service jobs and low unemployment. Marry those realities with affordable housing, beautiful cityscapes and good air quality and it's easy to understand why, in 2008, *MoneySense Magazine* named it the best place to live in the entire country.

> **IF THE LORD IS SENDING US PEOPLE FROM DIFFERENT NATIONS, WE'RE GOING TO MINISTER TO THEM.**

André Constant, 57, has witnessed the growth of Gatineau. As pastor of Église chrétienne du Plateau for more than three decades, he's also seen changes in his city bring transformation to his church.

"We built [in the church's current location] in 2006, and when we arrived here we were 180 people," he says. "Eight years later we're over 300. We've almost doubled. Our big growth is immigrants. Mainly Africans and Haitians. Now, we're close to 40 percent immigrants. For a while I was praying and wondering, 'Lord, are you going to save some people from Quebec too?'" But Constant was quick to conclude, "If the Lord is sending us people from different nations, we're going to minister to them."

The proof is in the church's motto: "Praising God in diversity," and in the diverse faces and cultures represented in the pews. There's more evidence in the small flags that grace the walls of the lobby; one flag for each country of origin represented among the people, 24 in all, 10 from African countries alone.

Constant is not looking backward. He is enthusiastic about the changes. "I say to the church that it's a foretaste of heaven. We won't be separated in different churches. We're going to praise the Lord together—in different tongues. We may as well get started and get some practice," he says with a chuckle.

That doesn't mean it's all been smooth sailing. Determining how to integrate so many new immigrants into the church hasn't been easy. Many come from cultures where going to church on Sunday is just what you do. Transforming mere churchgoers into genuine disciples of Jesus has been the church's key challenge.

Responding effectively to the needs of new immigrants has been another. While Nyiraneza and her children benefitted from help arising out of informal relationships, three years ago, Église chrétienne du Plateau has moved toward more intentional ministry, establishing Comité d'entraide, best translated "Mutual Aid Committee."

Nathalie Rochette is the team's coordinator, providing oversight to five others—all first-generation immigrants. "We gather information [on the needs of newcomers] as we participate in the life of the church," Rochette explains.

In the same way that relationship led to extending care for Nyiraneza and her family, it is relationship that leads to caring for the needs of others. Team members keep their eyes and ears open, demonstrating genuine interest and concern. "I work in the nursery on Sundays," Rochette says, as an example, "so I get to know the families with very young babies. I get to see if everything's fine. I ask questions. That's how we gather information."

And when the mutual aid team learns of a need, they set out to meet it. It is that simple. And that complex.

"We often reach people when the woman is pregnant. We have six people pregnant in the church right now. When the baby is born, we will visit with meals and just by talking to them, we'll see if there's something else we can do. We can't respond to all of the needs, but we can connect them with other resources."

The team has focused on meeting practical needs, ranging from offering transportation and help registering children for school, to assistance with minor repairs, help painting a new apartment and locating needed winter coats, beds or other furniture.

But also, "We often go to visit them," says Rochette. "We pray with them. Sometimes, there's a family reunification. We'll provide the meals for an entire week to ease the welcome. We'll give grocery tickets and go grocery shopping with them; it's a good chance to get to know them and answer their questions—what to pack in a school lunch, for example. Sometimes we'll call them through the week just to encourage them and say hi as a way for them to know they're not alone. When they arrive, they can feel really alone."

Chat with Rochette for even a short while, and it's clear she's the right person for the job. Making new friends, easing the transition for newcomers to her community and her church is more than an act of service—it's a passion.

"I have this feeling that when [new immigrants] arrive, they have lots on their shoulders," she says. "They feel heavy and they need that to be a bit lighter. We want to help in that way. It's good for their spiritual health too."

Providing such help, extending a warm welcome to immigrants, has also been good for the spiritual health of Église chrétienne du Plateau. "Church is more than programs that have to be run and things to be done" says Constant. "It's people. And the immigrants remind us to take care of the people."

EGLISE CHRETIENNE DU PLATEAU
118 boulevard du Plateau, Gatineau, QC | Ph. 819.771.7871
www.ecdp.ca

MORE TO EXPLORE

 Religious attendance is actually higher among immigrants to Canada than among the general public, a fact that has remained fairly stable over the last few decades.

 Compare these numbers:

- 43% of immigrants reported in 2011 that they attended religious services at least once a month, the same share as in 1998.

- By contrast, 22% of native-born Canadians said in 2011 that they attended religious services at least once a month, down from 31% in 1998.

Pew Research Center. "Canada's Changing Religious Landscape." Religion & Public Life Project. June 27, 2013. **www.pewforum.org**

GANDER,
NEWFOUNDLAND

FURNISHING WITH
LOVE IN GANDER

23. FURNISHING WITH LOVE IN GANDER

In the hall of Evangel Church at 59 Elizabeth Drive, Gander, Newfoundland, there are a few of your mother's end tables, circa 1975.

There's also one of those red plastic cars, the type that kids move with foot-power, like the Flintstones did. There are beds and boxes, lamps and lights, rich burgundy and moss green chairs balanced on a white couch that is itself stacked on a floral one.

This is the storage room at the end of this church's hall, the space that used to house the stage that used to host raucous Vacation Bible School presentations. The stage was ripped out a couple of years ago and the space made open and wide to store the gently used and ready to be reused furniture that puts legs on Evangel's motto: "A Heart for People."

That tagline, with a sketch of a cross and a heart beside a large sky-blue photo of a hand reaching out to help another, is emblazoned on the white cube truck parked out back.

That truck delivers furniture to those in need in a community already made globally famous by its care for others. For who could forget on September 11, 2001, when 38 US-bound airplanes were diverted to Gander, how the town rose to the occasion—as everyone knew a Newfoundland town would— offering tender care to the more than 6000 weary and heartbroken travellers stranded there.

That's just what places like Gander do.

The heart of love and hospitality—that practical-as-it-can-get care for others—beats strong at Evangel Church. Ralph Benson is pastor of this Pentecostal congregation. The furniture ministry itself started "very simply," he says, with the needs of a young single mom.

"She had nothing. Someone in the church brought that to our attention." People donated a couch, then dishes, then more. "We got this person set up," says Benson. "Once that happened, we thought 'Wow, that was easy to do.'"

And the rest is furniture ministry history.

"We realized this is a great way to help people," says Benson.

There was no shortage of folks needing help. After all, the typical Canadian pattern has been that if the rest of the country is hurting, Newfoundland is likely in agony. If finances are a shifting stat causing concern elsewhere, they are a mighty force to be reckoned with here.

Word spread through the community to those with furniture to give—and those who needed to receive. The local news stations picked up the story. "I would have been afraid if I'd known what it would grow to be. But I didn't know," says Benson. At first, it was volunteers using their own pick-up trucks to deliver furniture. The church bought its own truck. Then more furniture came, so storage space was needed. That's when they tore down the stage, knocked down some walls and slapped up shelving.

The phone started to ring. Daily. The church applied to the government for funding and received a grant to purchase an even larger, new cube truck. Their old one is now stuffed with more furniture to give away.

They have funds to hire a coordinator, because they really, really need one. They manage waiting lists of people needing particular items at particular times. Sometimes people need everything. There was that one single father who had custody of his three kids and one empty apartment. He had nothing. He left the door unlocked for the church one morning when he left for work. That dad returned home to a fully furnished apartment, right down to plates in the kitchen, cutlery in the drawers and toys in the kids' rooms.

"The town of Gander," says Benson, "they know about us in a positive way. They believe in us. They want to help us do what we are doing. If someone has a secondhand couch, the word is on the street." Benson laughs as he recounts one woman who had a couch to give away and mentioned it to a friend who advised: "Give it to the Pentecostals!"

Justin Preston was a single dad, also with three young kids—who owned just about nothing—when he saw a flyer about the furniture ministry. He called. They came. With a couch, a washer and dryer, beds, mattresses, dressers. "Everything," says Preston. Including, eventually, an invitation to church. Preston said yes to church, yes to faith, yes to parenting classes and yes to volunteering with the ministry. Life has changed dramatically for Preston and his kids. "God can change people. I was a hardcore person. It changed me," says Preston.

And it all started, he says, "with getting furniture from the church."

Now, in Preston's role as a volunteer, he routinely sees people far worse off than he ever was. "Looking at the state of people's houses, they have nothing. And when I say nothing, I mean nothing. I lived in Gander for eight years and I have never seen people in such a hard state," he says. "And to see that the church would give them everything they need? And the looks on people's faces?"

> I WOULD HAVE BEEN AFRAID IF I'D KNOWN WHAT IT WOULD GROW TO BE. BUT I DIDN'T KNOW.

Both Preston and his pastor speak of significant church growth because of the furniture ministry. Which of course is not why they do what they are doing, but it's very nice for people with a heart to proclaim the Gospel to see people responding to God's provision.

A few years ago, the federal government searched through Gander for a nonprofit organization willing to accept the ownership and responsibility of two vacated army houses.

They finally approached Evangel because everyone else took a pass. Evangel agreed and entered the world of transitional housing. That means they accept families for an 18-month housing rehabilitation period. During that time the church partners with the families to help them grow into reliable, rent-paying tenants who will be able to find permanent housing. There are committees to clean and repair the houses (with the church providing the furniture, of course), and committees to work with the residents on life skills like budgeting, life issues and parenting.

It's been a lot of work and a bit of a gamble. "No good to have them there for a year and a half, and move them out if we don't work with them. When they move out we have to recommend them," says Benson. While there's nothing perfect here, he adds, "We are learning. We are not giving up on these people. I'm hoping we will get more of these houses."

And all of this sometimes-complicated presence in the community is just "the simplicity of the Gospel," says Benson. "It's the simplicity of what the Church is supposed to be. We've been so legalistic and so rigid. The simplicity of what we are doing, of getting rid of religion and being more real. It has exploded for us in this place."

It's all so obvious in the Word, he says. "It's the way of Jesus. How did we miss this?"

Evangel Church is currently involved in a building project, expanding their facilities to make room for their new congregants. Their dream includes a furniture warehouse so they can expand their ministry even beyond Gander.

EVANGEL CHURCH
59 Elizabeth Drive, Gander, NL | Ph. 709.256.4762
www.evangelgander.ca

MORE TO EXPLORE

 Churches need to begin to respond to shifting Canadian realities by knowing their community and knowing what the need is, says Benson. "God will bring about what needs to happen in that local church and community."

 Although he could not be more enthusiastic about Evangel's furniture ministry, "Don't duplicate," Benson says. "We don't have a formula here. It's so simple. It's just reaching people where they are outside of the Church."

 "People still believe in God, but they don't believe in the Church. We have to change that perception," says Benson. "That is a big challenge."

IT'S MORE THAN JUST A MEAL

24. IT'S MORE THAN JUST A MEAL

"In the Maritimes, we love to eat," says Michael Caines, rector of Church of the Resurrection in Grand Bay-Westfield, New Brunswick, just outside Saint John. The mission statement of the parish (an amalgamation whose real name is a mouthful in itself: Parish of the Nerepis and St. John, Church of the Resurrection St. Paul's & St. Peter's) is "Jesus Centered. In the Community. For the Community." Living that mission statement out has involved food (lots of it) and empowering the church's youth in a new and profound way.

On the last Wednesday evening of each month, the church's youth group, together with other parishioners, make the 15-minute drive into uptown Saint John to serve a homemade, nutritious meal to folks Caines describes as "people struggling in some capacity, who need a hot meal and sense of community." This is an area of Saint John full of struggling people— it boasts one of the poorest per capita demographics in Canada twinned with the highest teen pregnancy rate.

The invitation to the church to be involved in the already established "Outflow" meal program arrived at just the right moment for a congregation looking for ways to become valuable to its community. "We got the whole youth group involved," says Caines. "We want to be the kind of church that is out in the community and Jesus-centred. This was a no-brainer opportunity to get involved. We prepare enough to feed 60-plus people. We serve, but then we sit down and eat with everyone there."

There were some nerves at first, with youth not used to walking the bridge between those who have and those who have not. Caines helped solve that by plunking down into a seat himself and striking up conversations with the people who were served at the meal. "You lead by example. You go first. What they see you doing gives the youth the confidence to do it themselves," he says. "In our parish of Grand Bay, poverty in your face is not an issue we have. It was a cultural leap. You have to just go for it," he says. "The kids follow suit. Some of them have really launched on to this."

Patrick Doyle, 13, is one of them. "A lot of people, when they look at a church, think about sitting in pews and listening to a sermon. This shows the church is more—it's about helping others and being a big family. It shows our church is there for other people," says Patrick. He believes serving at Outflow with his youth group has given him a sense of purpose and belonging. "For a while it was really just my routine of getting up and going to youth group. It was fun but it wasn't anything new. It's really changed my outlook on a lot of things."

There is a before-and-after-Outflow vibe with Patrick. There was the sitting around and not doing too much phase of this teen's life. That was before. Now, "I get to do something that helps other people and it feels really empowering to know I can help someone. I get to go and help someone in need and it feels really great," he says. Patrick remembers being intimidated the first time the youth group went and actually walked around an uptown square looking for those in need. "Within a week I knew most of them and I was excited to be there."

There is a growing confidence in Patrick, a confidence in himself and in his church's ability to make a difference.

The church's involvement in Outflow energized the entire congregation to explore other ministry opportunities right under their nose, or right on the edge of their property, where cucumbers, tomatoes, beans, carrots, potatoes and more now populate a new community garden. One-third of the produce goes directly to the food bank. The church invited community members to plant a row for themselves and to get involved in the weeding and harvesting of the garden as a whole. "We said, 'Come here and use this plot for your garden.' That was it," says Caines. The result is a partnership that brings Christians together with other community members who may feel more comfortable with a hoe than a hymnbook.

Partnership appeals to Caines. Outflow, for example, is a partnership of 30 churches, each taking one night a month. "I'm 100% for partnerships with other churches. Why try to go out on your own and reinvent the wheel?" he asks. "There are Kingdom things happening that we can join in. We don't need to make a name for ourselves. We just want to serve."

> THERE ARE KINGDOM THINGS HAPPENING THAT WE CAN JOIN IN. WE DON'T NEED TO MAKE A NAME FOR OURSELVES. WE JUST WANT TO SERVE.

Engaging in active, hands-on ministry has changed Patrick Doyle and the other youth at this church with the very long name. They have become youth whose faith and confidence have grown through the doing of the Gospel. Patrick tells of one particularly memorable evening at Outflow. "There was a man who came up to me after the meal," he remembers. "He said he really wanted to thank us. He said that that night was going to be his last night, but seeing us gave him strength to go on.

"I realized then," says Patrick, "that it's more than just a meal."

IT'S MORE THAN JUST A MEA_

> "This church modelled in an authentic and real way how to build community. Community is a two-way street where we have to learn to receive and to give. They promote a large Kingdom perspective where they intentionally have partnered with others."
>
> **– Matt Wilks**,
> Team Leader, Canadian Youth Worker

PARISH OF THE NEREPIS AND ST. JOHN, CHURCH OF THE RESURRECTION, ST. PAUL'S & ST. PETER'S
20 Macdonald Avenue, Grand Bay, NB | Ph. 506.738.3474
www.churchoftheresurrection.ca

MORE TO EXPLORE

 The Homeless Hub of Canada is a one-stop resource site for information about homelessness across Canada. You can search by community to find out facts like how many people stay in shelters, rental vacancy rates and average income in your part of the country. **www.homelesshub.ca.**

 A Rocha Canada has a Community Garden Network that includes instructions and information on how to get started and a way to register your garden for ongoing encouragement The network includes an online forum and Facebook page.
www.arocha.ca/communitygardens

 A case study on youth and volunteerism in Canada revealed that including youth in planning and strategy sessions is "integral to receiving their support," and better engagement from youth comes with better education on the impact of their involvement. Volunteer Canada, 'Engaging Youth Effectively'.
www.volunteer.ca

WINNIPEG,
MANITOBA

MAKING DIGITAL CONNECTIONS

25. MAKING DIGITAL CONNECTIONS

There's something about knowing people have actually prayed for you that feels so much better than just hearing the often-spoken-but-all-too-often-quickly-forgotten promise: "I'll pray for you."

Hearing that promise may provide a moment's solace, but knowing that someone has prayed—receiving visible proof they've done so—is affirming, encouraging and faith building. Gratitude buoys your spirit. Hope infuses your soul. You realize, whatever your struggle or burden, you're not facing it alone.

This is the value of the online prayer community offered through the website of Grant Memorial Church (grantmemorial.ca) in Winnipeg, Manitoba: those who post prayer requests receive ongoing, visible proof that people are indeed praying.

The proof comes in the form of a short, simple statement in unadorned blue text that appears beside each request posted: "Prayed for 10 times," or "Prayed for 31 times," or for the most recent posts "Prayed for 1 time," the numeric tally increasing with each click of a navy button marked "I prayed for this," alongside every request. Those who have posted requests can do so anonymously, and may opt in to receive a notification each time someone indicates they have prayed. It is a beautiful system: secure, responsive, easy to use and designed to make the most of the spontaneous empathy and goodwill that often motivate promises to pray. And it is a model that takes advantage of the fact that people sitting in front of a computer screen are ideally positioned to actually pause for a few minutes—or even a few seconds—to pray.

The online prayer community is just one component of this church's recently overhauled, carefully planned and intuitively designed website, which includes links to church social media accounts, blogs, a treasure trove of downloadable resources, links to register for church events, forms people can fill out to receive a home or hospital visit, opportunities to give online, and much more. The process of developing an online catalogue for church library resources is underway.

"Current technology has transformed the way people find information," says Angi McCarty, coordinator of communications and marketing at Grant Memorial. "[The Internet] is how people are finding information, connecting and engaging now. If we don't go in this direction, we won't have a church."

A former journalist, McCarty works with an entire team of people—both staff and volunteers—devoted to keeping their church and Linden Christian School (which is affiliated with the church) on the leading edge of technology. It is a commitment that touches on more than just their website.

"This year we launched a new online bulletin designed for handheld devices," says McCarty. While the church still produces a print version of the weekly bulletin, McCarty says their hope is that people will use their devices in the service to follow the bulletin and take notes. Hyperlinks in the bulletin direct visitors to the church's website. Ultimately, the move to digital bulletins will help to save paper and reduce print costs.

McCarty and her colleagues have also helped develop a digital mission magazine. Their expertise and creativity have led to a digital outdoor sign, indoor digital signage throughout the large church-and-school complex, touch screens for a world mission display and to advertise volunteer opportunities and to

SHIFTING STATS

> CURRENT TECHNOLOGY HAS TRANSFORMED THE WAY PEOPLE FIND INFORMATION...IF WE DON'T GO IN THIS DIRECTION, WE WON'T HAVE A CHURCH.

allow people to sign up for events. There are iPads in the foyer for online giving, e-newsletters, and a digital constituent database. The church hosts educational simulcast events that draw crowds of up to 200 people.

McCarty acknowledges that not every church has access to the vast resources she and her team have been blessed to steward. She is humble when asked to reflect on the changes she's seen in her eight years in the job. "We haven't got it all figured out by any means," she concedes. "It's all about incremental change. Step by step. Each year we add something new or try to become just a little more advanced in how we communicate."

*

At 31, Chris Wyllie is one of those raised-on-technology, largely self-taught guys who quickly becomes the go-to person for anyone and everyone with a tech problem. He serves as technical coordinator, overseeing the audio-visual needs of both the 900-student school and Grant Memorial.

"Most churches might have youth and their Sunday services and a few other events in the week," he says. "But we have four chapel services a week, plus two Sunday services, and a bunch of other events—it's almost 24/7. I was hired to run and help produce the events."

Wyllie believes there are two important considerations for using technology in the church: how it's used for the benefit of attendees, and how it's used for outreach. "When people walk into the room, that's one thing," he says. "But how we capture the service and put it online for the non-attendees to see, that's the technology that's come in the last three years.

"Churches are looking at getting the message out to people who aren't even in the building, so they can come to know the Lord through the messages online, or they can look at the church and find a family and want to come."

That's increasingly the future, as far as Wyllie is concerned. "We're going to be working on creating content," he says. "And that content will be used online and targeted to non-Christians in hopes to grow not just our church, but *the* Church. We want to use our resources to impact God's Kingdom, not just grow our attendance."

GRANT MEMORIAL CHURCH
877 Wilkes Avenue, Winnipeg, MB | Ph. 204.989.6740
www.grantmemorial.ca

SHIFTING STATS

MORE TO EXPLORE

 Just over two-thirds (67 percent) of Canadians who used the Internet in 2012 visited social networking sites like Facebook or Twitter, up from 58 percent in 2010. Ladurantaye, Steve. "Canada tops globe in Internet usage." *The Globe and Mail*, March 1, 2012. **www.theglobeandmail.com**

 Increasingly, Canadians are accessing the Internet with phones and other handheld devices. And we've got a lot of them! According to the Canadian Wireless Telecommunications Association, Canadian wireless phone subscribers alone number over 27 million; this in a country with a total population of just over 35 million. Canadian Wireless Telecommunications Association. *CWTA Facts & Figures 2013*. **www.cwta.ca**

 According to research out of the U.S., seven out of 10 practicing Christians of the Millennial generation (those born from the early 1980s to the early 2000s) read Scripture on a screen, demonstrating just how broadly digital trends are shaping this generation. Barna Research Group. "How Technology is Changing Millennial Faith," Barna: Millennials, October 15, 2013. **www.barna.org**

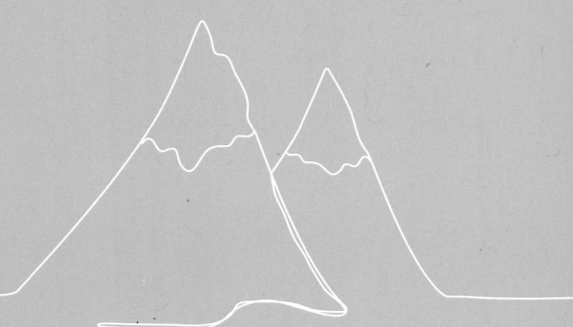

26. JESUS ISN'T ONLY FOR WHITE PEOPLE

The story of The Life Centre in Abbotsford, British Columbia really begins with the story of its pastor, Bindu Jaswinder Sidhu.

Born in India's Punjab region, Sidhu's family immigrated to Canada when he was three years old. The family was Sikh. Like countless immigrants before them and after, they chose to settle in an area that bore some sense of the familiar.

Located in the heart of the Fraser Valley in B.C.'s lower mainland, Abbotsford couldn't be more different from India. But agriculture is key to the economy here, and that may have been an attraction when the area's first Sikhs began to arrive in the early 1900s from the Punjab (where most of the world's Sikh population lives)—an area so fertile it's known as the breadbasket of India.

Today this city is home to the oldest existing Sikh temple in North America. One out of every five Abbotsford residents is South Asian. And the Census Metropolitan Area (CMA) encompassing the city has the highest percentage—at 17 percent—of people belonging to the Sikh faith of all CMAs in Canada.

When the Sidhu family settled here, they chose the west side of town, on a street rapidly transitioning from white faces to brown, where saffron orange turbans were the norm. Sidhu's mother prepared family meals with dishes like aloo paratha, butter chicken and saag, by shopping at neighbourhood Punjabi grocery stores.

But the local churches became reminders of how white the neighbourhood used to be. More than 30 years later, Sidhu remembers that as a boy, "the only time I saw white people come into our neighbourhood was for church." The white Christians came on Sundays, and then they went away again until the next Sunday. The perception in the Punjabi community, says Sidhu, was that "Jesus is for white people."

"There was a church in Abbotsford that was one of the largest churches in all of Western Canada," he reflects. "I didn't even know it existed."

When Sidhu came to faith in Christ at the age of 19, then married a Caucasian woman and sensed God calling him into full-time ministry, he became convinced that there had to be a better way of doing church. Some people from his community began to call him a "coconut," he says, "brown on the outside and white on the inside," but Sidhu is convinced, "You can speak Punjabi and love Jesus. You can eat the food and love Jesus. You can listen to Punjabi music and love Jesus."

"For me, the saddest thing to see is segregation in the city," he says. "Christ came that the nations might be grafted into the Kingdom. The Church is probably the last place in our city where's there's significant integration of cultures. Sunday morning is the most segregated hour in Abbotsford. All of our churches are white. And to me that's heartbreaking because that's not the message of the Gospel."

In 2006 Sidhu led the team that planted The Life Centre, with the purpose of being a church that would love God and reflect the community. They meet for worship in a building situated on the west side of town in a predominantly Punjabi neighbourhood.

"Our goal as a church is to love our neighbour," he explains. "I really believe that we're here by God's grace. The key to proclaiming the Gospel among the nations is God's people being friends with the nations."

Sidhu says there's far more diversity in west Abbotsford than in the east. "This is where the nations are. So this is where we need to be."

With 19 different countries of origin represented among those who call The Life Centre their spiritual home, the congregation is definitely diverse. And they've incorporated a number of practices into their worship that celebrate that diversity.

> THE KEY TO PROCLAIMING THE GOSPEL AMONG THE NATIONS IS GOD'S PEOPLE BEING FRIENDS WITH THE NATIONS.

Each week, "we open the service in a different language," Sidhu explains. "We just rotate through them. Last week we prayed in Korean."

The congregation also sings hymns and contemporary songs in other languages, incorporates instruments from different cultures into their music, and follows the African tradition of literally dancing their tithes, gifts and food bank offerings to the front of the church each week.

Baby dedications are joyous, boisterous celebrations. Indian music plays while congregants do a Bhangra dance, arms raised high, around the doting parents and their baby. And with a high percentage of mixed-race marriages in the congregation, church small groups have studied such practical topics as "Raising Kids in Two Cultures."

Elaine Im immigrated to Canada from South Korea about the time The Life Centre was born. The first time she visited the church, "I saw all these different flags up at the front," she remembers. Then, glimpsing her country's flag, she became emotional. "It was awesome," she says.

In a city with several Korean churches, Im says she settled on The Life Centre because of its intercultural approach.

Ike Agawin came to Canada from the Philippines. Working on a PhD at ACTS Seminaries, he's engaged in a comparative study of multicultural churches in the province's Lower Mainland, and has chosen to make The Life Centre his church home. He says worship becomes more natural and more intuitive when people worship in their heart language. "There's a value in every culture's worship," he says. "Revelation 7 says that people from every tribe, tongue and nation will be worshipping the Lord. We're living that future now."

> "Who is my neighbour? That is the question all of our churches need to ask themselves, and all of us as followers of Jesus need to answer."
> – **Diane Marshall**, Registered Marriage and Family Therapist, Institute for Family Living

THE LIFE CENTRE
c/o 35553 Tweedsmuir Drive, Abbotsford, BC | Ph. 778.808.4668
www.thelc.net

SHIFTING STATS

MORE TO EXPLORE

 Many churches are multicultural. But The Life Centre has taken things a step further by adopting a truly intercultural approach to worship.

 One in every five people who live in Canada was born outside of the country. Statistics Canada. "Immigration and Ethnocultural Diversity in Canada," p. 4 **www12.statcan.gc.ca**

 While two-thirds of Canadian residents identify as affiliating with Christianity, "growing proportions" of the population identify with non-Christian religions. Statistics Canada. "Immigration and Ethnocultural Diversity in Canada," p. 20 – 21. **www12.statcan.gc.ca**

NORTH BAY,
ONTARIO

FLOURISHING FAMILIES
AND FRIENDSHIPS

27. FLOURISHING FAMILIES AND FRIENDSHIPS

On a Thursday evening in late September 2014—when the days were growing shorter and the leaves had begun to change their summer greens to reds and golds—Caroline Harrison heard the weather forecast for the approaching weekend. Then she posted a friendly, impromptu callout to the closed Facebook group for Trinity Families. "EVERYTHING IS AWESOME!" her invitation began, "Outdoor movie night at the Harrisons."

Two days later, 40 people assembled on the large back deck of the Harrison home. It was one of those beautiful early fall evenings, cool but clear. As the sun set, pyjama-clad children snuggled down on camping mattresses with pillows and blankets in front of a large bedsheet serving as a movie screen erected especially for the occasion. Together with their parents (who perched on nearby benches or settled into lawn chairs) they enjoyed chips and popcorn, pop and *The Lego Movie* under the stars. It was a celebration of family and friendship, and a last shout-out to summer.

It was also a typical gathering of Trinity Families—loose, casual and relatively spontaneous, a formula that has served the group of families from Trinity United Church in North Bay, Ontario well.

"It took very little planning," says Harrison. The event was so last minute, she concedes, they didn't even have time to announce it at church. "We just threw the invitation up on Facebook and got enough responses that we knew people were coming. It was fun.

"We all acknowledge that it doesn't have to be perfect," she adds, "that life is busy. It doesn't have to be a lot of work for people. We just keep it very casual."

That approach is in direct response to the needs of time-strapped contemporary families, says Lisa Blais, Children, Family and Youth Minister at Trinity, and it's also one of the keys to the group's success. "They're casual. Loosely structured. Often on a whim. There's not a lot of planning.

"Sometimes we're scrambling at the last minute. But we get it done. We don't go through committees and take ten meetings to decide what we're going to do. We just do it."

Just doing it is in this group's DNA. Trinity Families arose organically in the spring of 2010, says Marcel MacDonald, who has become the group's coordinator. "People try different churches. At some point, there were newer families coming and we were talking and wondered, 'How do we get them to want to stay?'"

What they concluded was, "the same way we did," says MacDonald, who explains that people most often decide to stay at a new church because of relationships. "You get to know someone and you start hanging out together."

Some 22 to 25 Trinity Families hang out each year, taking trips to a pumpkin patch in fall and a maple syrup festival in spring. At Christmas, they drag couches and easy chairs out to the curb in front of the church for the children when the Santa Claus Parade marches by, and they serve hot chocolate and popcorn to bystanders. They try to meet monthly, but don't sweat the details.

"This group is a little loosey-goosey," concedes Harrison. "If an event doesn't happen for three months, well, then we pick it up again afterwards."

But don't make the mistake of thinking people aren't invested in this group. The friendship bonds that have developed among the members of Trinity Families are so strong that the parents sometimes get together—to play board games or just to visit over a potluck dinner or dessert and coffee—without the kids. Just for fun.

> SOMETIMES WE'RE SCRAMBLING AT THE LAST MINUTE. BUT WE GET IT DONE. WE DON'T GO THROUGH COMMITTEES...TO DECIDE WHAT WE'RE GOING TO DO. WE JUST DO IT.

"I think it's really important to be able to get away from the kids once in awhile," says Mac-Donald, "to be able to socialize as adults. Because you might meet over your kids, but if that's the only time you meet, you don't have anything in common but your kids. So we have a network of babysitters. If anybody needs a sitter they can let us know. Sometimes, people will share a babysitter and help each other out by splitting the cost."

Blais says the fact that Trinity Families occasionally holds adults-only events is a key to the group's popularity. "I think that's been really integral to solidifying friendships with the parents. Sometimes when you're doing things as a family, you're spending time just with your own family," she says, "and you're having parallel conversations with other people. But having the opportunity to connect on an adult level has been really good."

Darlene Laferriere takes her two school-aged grandchildren to Trinity Families. She goes to the adults-only events too. "It's a safe place to have fun," she says. "And for my generation, it takes the place of what we used to do in our neighbourhoods.

"Children once played together in neighbourhoods. And our parents got together and had parties. But neighbourhoods don't function that way anymore."

Wes Johnson and his wife Karen say they chose to make Trinity United Church their home after checking out a lot of different area churches, precisely because of the sense of community they found there. He says Trinity Families has been "really important for my family. I think it's important to have a community wherever you are. We were looking for a place where our kids would be excited to go." The Families group turned out to be icing on a delicious cake that consisted of a great Sunday School program, children's choir, excellent annual Vacation Bible School and more.

Blais says the group has also helped to reverse the greying trend experienced in a lot of mainline congregations. "On Sunday mornings, a lot of families are doing other activities, and they're not always able to come to church," she says. "This was sort of a response to the question of, how do we maintain our faith and connections outside of church?"

Blais sums up the philosophy of ministry at Trinity, "We are staying current and relevant to the way families are today."

TRINITY UNITED CHURCH
111 McIntyre Street E, North Bay, ON | Ph. 705.474.3310
www.trinitynorthbay.ca

MORE TO EXPLORE

As work hours rise, time for other priorities—like church and family—falls. Statistics Canada tells us that workers spent an average of 45 minutes less per day with family members in 2005 than they did 20 years earlier. CBC News. "Longer Work Day Cutting Into Family Time: Study." February 13, 2007. **www.cbc.ca**

Elaine Sauer, bishop of the Evangelical Lutheran Church in Canada, has observed that her denomination is seeing fewer and fewer families with children in Sunday morning worship. She says: "As the norm becomes two-income families, people are using their Sundays as additional days to do other activities as families, or regular or additional chores that couldn't be done during the week. Longhurst, John. "The Church and Family Changing Demographics." *Winnipeg Free Press*, November 17, 2012. **www.winnipegfreepress.com**

Through observation of current family trends and awareness of the needs of contemporary families, Trinity United Church has encouraged a unique family ministry to grow and flourish that is attracting new families to their congregation.

CHARLIE LAKE,
BRITISH
COLUMBIA

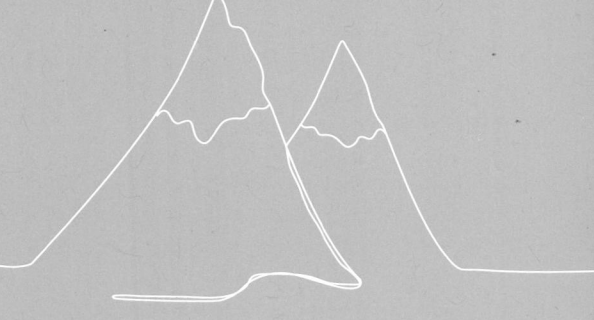

SHOTS AND SWAPS

28. SHOTS AND SWAPS

Once upon a time, a small, rural church was erected just off the Alaska Highway in northeastern British Columbia. Overlooking scenic Charlie Lake (just outside the region's largest city of Fort St. John), Charlie Lake Community Church was a labour of love. Originally a ski lodge, volunteers had dismantled the building log-by-log, then hauled it a half-hour away to its current location. Each piece of wood was painstakingly sanded, cleaned and reassembled. It took years.

But the vision, commitment and energy—the sheer stamina—it took to complete the building would serve as a model for this congregation as they labour to respond to the needs of their surrounding community.

Charlie Lake's Sunday bulletin reads like those of innumerable other small churches across the country, with announcements about small groups, moms-and-tots Bible studies, potluck dinners and men's breakfasts. But the ongoing question, says senior pastor Alfred Reschke has been "How do we do outreach?" undergirded by the more fundamental questions of "Who are we as a church, and how are we going to relate to the community?"

In an era when the church is no longer the focal point of community life, and in a region where people live not streets but miles apart, these are not easy questions to answer.

The church has held Vacation Bible School, but found that sometimes they were serving more families from other churches than non-church families. They've held community BBQs but "the response wasn't great," says Reschke. They helped establish the only Canadian chapter of the Oilfield Christian Fellowship, but the workers' long hours and busy schedules made meetings so difficult that they were eventually cancelled altogether. They've rented large inflatable bouncy toys for children at the local fall fair and wrestled with the feasibility of being involved in the community's winter festival, but "in the end we decided we couldn't get enough manpower together."

Charlie Lake Community Church is not alone. Their story surely resonates in the hearts and minds of church leaders across the country. But perseverance often pays off. And recently, the congregation struck pay dirt by hosting two very different events.

Northeastern British Columbia is something of a hunter's paradise. But Fort St. John has grown rapidly through an influx of young families who've moved north to take advantage of the security and prosperity offered by jobs in the oil patch. Raised elsewhere, many of the young men and women who head up those families have little or no exposure to guns.

Recognizing this lack of experience to be an unmet need in their community, the church decided to offer them gun training. In his spare time, Reschke is a firearms instructor. "I do two courses a month where I'm teaching on the weekends," he says. "There is no issue of these courses being full. Every single weekend. As people spend a little time up here they soon realize that many of the people they work with are into hunting. That's just part of the dynamic of the community," he says. "And there are so many people out here that are new to shooting, they don't have a place to connect."

So Charlie Lake Community Church created a partnership with a local gun club. The congregation hosted a free family BBQ and trap shoot (an event during which people shoot at clay targets) at the firing range immediately following their morning worship service on a Sunday afternoon in June 2014. Designed to be a safe, non-threatening and family-friendly atmosphere, members of the congregation invited friends from the community. "In the end, a little over 150 people showed up," says Reschke, who estimates more than a quarter of those who came were not affiliated with the congregation. Moms and dads and kids as young as four years old enjoyed an afternoon of fun and instruction.

> IT WAS NEAT TO SEE HOW PEOPLE WHO PREVIOUSLY HAD ZERO INTEREST IN CHURCH CAME OUT AND RUBBED SHOULDERS WITH CHURCH FOLKS.

"It was neat to see how people who previously had zero interest in church came out and rubbed shoulders with church folks," Reschke reflects.

Recently, a women's clothing and accessories swap, which took a bit of an unexpected turn, led to more of that shoulder rubbing.

It was the second year for the event, held the first time as a social outing for the women of the church. The original idea behind the swap was that women would arrive with outfits and accessories they no longer wanted, and leave with clothing, purses, jewelry and/or shoes that someone else had given away.

But, says organizer Natalie Braun, the first swap revealed "our church is very willing to give, but they don't want to come and get. Last year they took five or six huge bags of unwanted clothing to the thrift store."

As Braun began sorting through bags of donated items in the weeks leading up to the second annual evening event she realized "there was an abundance of nice clothes," more than would ever be needed by the women of the church alone.

"So that's when I started inviting other [non-church] people."

After advertising the event locally, Braun and a handful of volunteers set up the church basement as a women's clothing shop, where women could browse and then select items for free. "We had different tables set up for sweaters, tops and pants. Everything was organized by sizes," she explains. "We had clothing racks for blouses, a table for jewelry, a rack with scarves and purses. And I prettied up one corner with nicer dresses and skirts."

Tables and chairs, and a buffet with coffee and treats invited the "shoppers" to socialize.

Five minutes before they were scheduled to open their doors the first two shoppers arrived. They left before the evening was out with two green garbage bags each filled with clothing. Braun estimates some 30 women came, 80 percent of them not affiliated with the church. The volunteers worked hard to offer a luxury shopping experience. "We set up change rooms and brought them clothes," says Braun. One enthusiastic shopper didn't want the evening to end. So Braun told her, "Then just stay and let us serve you."

Billee-Jo Korfmann is a church member and mother to two young children. She says she enjoyed the swap not only for the clothes she was able to find—"It's a really easy way to change up the wardrobe a little bit"—but also for the social aspect. Besides, "I was able to take some things out of my closet that definitely didn't need to be there," she adds. "And I noticed none of them were there when I arrived at the exchange, so I know someone got them. And that made me very happy. They're not collecting dust anymore."

Braun is philosophical when asked why the most recent clothing swap was such a success. While finances are not an issue for many local families who have found employment opportunities through the oil patch, finances can still be an challenge, she says, for some families, like those headed by lone parents. Calling the event "a swap," rather than a free giveaway "might make it less awkward … a little less humbling or embarrassing," to come and get what you need, she says.

"It's expensive to buy clothes. And it feels nice to wear something new—even if it doesn't come with a tag on it."

CHARLIE LAKE COMMUNITY CHURCH
Box 639, Charlie Lake, BC | Ph. 250.785.1723
www.charlielakechurch.com

MORE TO EXPLORE

 Charlie Lake Community Church set out on their quest to meet the needs of their neighbours by first asking, "Who are we as a church, and how are we going to relate to our community?"

 Through a combination of persistence, trial and error, imagination and a willingness to innovate, Charlie Lake Community Church is discovering unique ways of both meeting—and meeting the needs of—their community.

 No matter where you live in Canada, one of the most significant culture-shapers is money. Ours is a consumer society, but that doesn't mean there isn't also great financial need. We're also debt-ridden. On average, Canadians spend more than $1.63 for every dollar they make. Statistics Canada. "National balance sheet and financial flow accounts, second quarter 2013."
www.statcan.gc.ca

HAY RIVER, NORTHWEST TERRITORIES

CAMPING IN PARADISE

29. CAMPING IN PARADISE

The video posted to Paradise Bible Camp's Facebook page in March 2014 is not what one could describe as a "typical" camp video. It contains sounds and images of giggling, active children, of course, but also talk of lynx meat, shots of children wielding hatchets and saws, and glimpses of a partly skinned and bloodied wolf carcass, the animal's mouth frozen agape in apparent end-of-life throes.

But then, Camp Paradise isn't a typical Christian camp. It is the only child-and-youth Bible camp in Canada's far North. The camp video was captured during a winter weekend program designed to teach local children to hunt, trap and fish.

The camp is located outside the tiny town of Hay River (population just over 3600) in the South Slave Lake region of the Northwest Territories. Here hunting, trapping and fishing aren't mere hobbies, but a way of life, and a vital part of the Aboriginal people's culture and tradition.

Before Camp Paradise opened for business in 2001, children from the Northwest Territories—who wanted a Christian camp experience—had to travel many hours south by a combination of boat, plane and/or roadway into British Columbia, Alberta or Saskatchewan to get it. But such travel is costly. So few children ever did.

Then a decade-and-a-half ago, a local man by the name of Bruce Domes had what he describes as "a vision" that someday children in the far North would be able to hear the Gospel in the same type of fun-filled Christian camp setting that their counterparts in Canada's more southern regions could.

"There's such a huge need here. Kids are just getting destroyed," says Domes, describing a Goliath-sized problem. Citing crime, endemic family dysfunction and addictions as examples of the challenges that constitute daily life for many young people, Domes says the Aboriginal culture in Canada's far North has largely been eroded. Colonialism, imperialism, unjust treatment by the federal and provincial governments, and the painful legacy of the residential school system have all taken a terrible toll.

Aboriginal people are "not living off the land anymore," says Domes. "They're not living the way they were intended to live up here."

In 2000, Domes bought and cleared six acres of land in Paradise Valley. Later, he transferred ownership of the land for a nominal sum to Jim Forsyth, a friend, on the condition that Forsyth would develop the property into a Christian camp.

He did. Today Camp Paradise runs year-round programming including children's, teens' and family camps that accommodate up to 40 campers each week throughout the summer.

*

If Camp Paradise is responding to Goliath-sized problems, it also has its David.

Jim Forsyth didn't act alone to develop Camp Paradise. At 65, he still works full time—he has all along—as a computer network analyst. His work developing the camp has been volunteer activity conducted in his off-hours and vacation time.

The church that played David is Forsyth's home church, Dene Pentecostal. From the beginning, it has had a key role in making this camp a reality. Located on the Northwest Territory's first Indian reservation, the Hay River Dene Reserve, the church's congregation swells to 20 people on a good Sunday. Two-thirds of them are from the Dene Nation.

"By far the majority are middle income," says Wes Dyck, the church's pastor, describing the congregation. "They're progres-

> ...JUST REALIZING IT'S AN OPPORTUNITY FOR THE CONGREGATION TO MAKE AN IMPACT ON KIDS AND YOUTH. AND THEY WANT TO DO THAT.

sive, hardworking, industrious people. Their homes are neat and well kept." In other words, they are careful and caring. And they were not only quick to embrace the vision for a Christian camp in their community, says Dyck, but they were eager to help make it happen.

Camp Paradise, he explains, "is providing a place here in the Northwest Territories for the kids from the communities to come to. There is nothing else up here," he adds. "It's the only camp of its style in the Northwest Territories, and obviously Jim being part of the church would have some effect on [the church's participation]. But the other part is just realizing it's an opportunity for the congregation to make an impact on kids and youth. And they want to do that."

Church members—including Dyck—serve on the camp's board of directors. Many in the small assembly have their own businesses and they've given time and resources to everything from construction to landscaping to camp ministry. "When there's work that needs to be done, people go out and help," explains Dyck.

Dene Pentecostal also makes a relatively substantial financial contribution to Camp Paradise each year—a contribution Forsyth says the camp depends on.

The influence of the camp extends far beyond Hay River. Campers come from communities like Fort Smith, Fort Simpson, Yellowknife, Rae-Edzo, Fort Resolution and Behchoko. "We've had kids come from as far away as Tulita, on the Mackenzie River," says Forsyth. "They have to come by boat for part of the trip because there are no roads. Up here, when we say 'our next door neighbour' we mean they're a three-to-five-hour drive away."

Isaac Simon, 14, of Fort Resolution is both a camper and a junior leader at Paradise Camp. He's made the journey there each summer for six consecutive years. "I like meeting new friends and getting to grow my relationship with God," he explains. "It's made a difference because I'm a stronger Christian now, and I have new friends and I get to have a fun time."

*

David was armed with a weapon. Countless individuals and teams of volunteers from myriad other churches serve as the five smooth stones and sling of this story. Allan and Shirley Clarkson of the Kamloops Vineyard Christian Fellowship in British Columbia are among them. The couple has given considerable time and energy to helping build the camp. "We built the office and the leader's cabin," says Allan referring to a team of volunteers. "Got the water lines in the first year. The second year we went up and got the plumbing done in the washrooms, the disposal areas and some of the electrical. The third year it was mostly painting. The fourth year we built a chapel."

For her part, Shirley would spend weeks shopping for the camp each year, prior to the start of the summer season, in order to take advantage of the sales and lower prices available down south.

But the Clarksons have also helped to raise considerable awareness of Paradise Camp and its ministry— drumming up support through their own local congregations, first in Grand Prairie, Alberta, and more recently in Kamloops.

To slay Goliath, David needed more than giant-sized courage and a weapon; he had faith that God would ultimately do what needed to be done. Forsyth and the Dene Pentecostal Church seem to possess a similar kind of trust. "To see God at work and know that it's His work and not my work definitely builds my faith," says Forsyth. "That's for sure."

DENE PENTECOSTAL CHURCH
Hay River, NT | Ph. 867.874.6622

MORE TO EXPLORE

 The terrible legacy of colonialism, imperialism and the residential schools has been that many Aboriginal peoples continue to struggle today against oppressive social ills.

 1,400,685 people had an Aboriginal identity in 2011, representing 4.3 percent of the total Canadian population. Aboriginal people accounted for 3.8 percent of the population enumerated in the 2006 Census, 3.3 percent in the 2001 Census and 2.8 percent in the 1996 Census. The largest numbers of Aboriginal people lived in Ontario and the Western provinces (Manitoba, Saskatchewan, Alberta and British Columbia). Aboriginal people made up the largest shares of the population of Nunavut and the Northwest Territories. Statistics Canada, *National Household Survey*: **www12.statcan.gc.ca**

 The Aboriginal population is young. Aboriginal children aged 14 and under made up 28 percent of the total Aboriginal population and 7 percent of all children in Canada. Non-Aboriginal children aged 14 and under represented 16.5 percent of the total non-Aboriginal population. Statistics Canada, National Household Survey: **www12.statcan.gc.ca**

CHESTERMERE, ALBERTA

BECOMING "MIGHTY NEIGHBOURLY"

30. BECOMING "MIGHTY NEIGHBOURLY"

Just three months after Catherine Taylor and her husband relocated from Ontario to the city of Chestermere, Alberta, they are already starting to feel at home, but not because it was an easy move to make.

The couple left behind family and friends and a lifetime of memories when they moved west to pursue employment opportunities. They feel so settled in large measure because of the warm welcome they received from their chosen community.

"A person came to our door with a little wooden crate filled with all kinds of information on the area and various different businesses, little goodies and treats," Taylor remembers. "It was really great. I've never had that before. In all the places I've lived, I've never had anyone say, 'Welcome to our area.'"

The Taylors were on the receiving end of the Mighty Neighbourly program, an innovative outreach project of Lake Ridge Community Church, a four-year-old church plant in Alberta's fastest growing municipality.

Lake Ridge pastor Evan Dewald is the mind behind Mighty Neighbourly. Friendly, outgoing and energetic, it's easy to understand why Dewald moved to the bedroom community (an overwhelming majority of the city's residents work in Calgary) in 2011, determined to make a difference in what was then just a town, but a town that had grown by 300 percent in a decade.

As a church planter, he says, one of his primary goals was to do his utmost to listen "to God, to ourselves—that is, what do I believe God is asking of me and what do I want—to each other, and to our community—that is, what is the community saying they need?"

Careful listening quickly convinced Dewald that one of the greatest needs of the booming town was for its residents to become involved citizens. He came by that knowledge firsthand. Not long after moving into Chestermere, the civic-minded Dewald sat on a city board called "The Inclusion Project."

"The group does everything from helping newcomers of different ethnicities acclimate into the community through various programs like reading, learning how to shop and cook in Canada, seminars and workshops on how to fill out citizenship forms," he says. "We also have to understand their culture. How can we prepare our historically white, English-speaking population to accept other ethnicities?"

It was an important question to wrestle with. According to city data, Chestermere has a total visible minority population higher than the rest of the province, and a higher percentage of first generation Canadians. The city, with its proximity to Calgary, its more affordable real estate and its lovely lake setting, has been something of a magnet.

"I hear all the time that people moved here for the small town feel," Dewald reflects. "I grew up in a town of 500 people. Believe me that 'feel' has nothing to do with numbers, and everything to do with the interaction we have with our neighbours. The more people who choose to get to know their neighbours, the better it will be for our community."

But one of the challenges of living in a small city that borders on a big one is that people tend to drive to the big one to take advantage of all it has to offer, rather than fully engaging in the life of their own community.

That observation led Dewald and a team of people to develop a proposal for Mightly Neighbourly, a church-run program that would ultimately receive substantial funding from Chestermere's United Way.

> I HEAR ALL THE TIME THAT PEOPLE MOVED HERE FOR THE SMALL TOWN FEEL...BELIEVE ME THAT 'FEEL' HAS NOTHING TO DO WITH NUMBERS, AND EVERYTHING TO DO WITH THE INTERACTION WE HAVE WITH OUR NEIGHBOURS.

The program has three components. The first promotes the city, welcomes new residents and encourages them to become involved. Church volunteers pay a brief, friendly visit to the homes of newcomers and deliver an attractive, handmade wooden crate filled with dozens of coupons from local businesses and gift items ranging from a pie or a potted flower to a free, year-long family membership to the local library.

The second component of the program involves handing out free, hearty, homemade frozen meals—everything from lasagna to cabbage rolls—prepared by church volunteers to families experiencing times of need. Dewald says that only six months in to the program they've distributed scores of welcome crates and hundreds of meals.

The final phase of the plan for Mighty Neighbourly will see the development of a special awards program highlighting great neighbours who engage in small acts of heroism.

Dewald says Christians ought to be among the first to encourage neighbourliness. "We believe we have a very hospitable God," he says. "If anyone is going to teach us what it means to be hospitable, it's God. So we wondered, how can what we know about God and community be translated here? How can we bless our neighbours?"

The real success of the program, he says, is that neighbours are indeed connecting with neighbours.

Patrice Pease concurs. A member of Lake Ridge, she and her husband moved to Chestermere only two years ago, but she was eager to become a volunteer in the program when she first heard about it. "It's really a great opportunity to get to know new people," she says of making the welcome visits. "It makes our community that much more tangible. People recognize you and say 'hello.'"

Pease has learned much about her new neighbours. "Everyone has a story," she says, "and that story is important and needs to be honoured. Our town is full of people who have just come to this country.

"And this is a movement of hospitality."

> "The need for community, for connection, is at the heart of who we are created to be as people made in the image of God. When family relationships break down, and people are marginalized from the warmth of love and acceptance, this church is reaching out in practical, life-affirming ways to their neighbours."
>
> – **Diane Marshall**,
> Registered Marriage and Family Therapist,
> Institute for Family Living

LAKE RIDGE COMMUNITY CHURCH
c/o 134 Rainbow Falls Drive, Chestermere, AB | Ph. 403.901.9200
www.lakeridgecommunity.com

SHIFTING STATS

MORE TO EXPLORE

 Writing in the January/February 2014 issue of *Faith Today* magazine, Regent College theologian John Stackhouse says, "The challenge for Canadian churches remains what it has always been—to connect with the felt needs of our neighbours." Through a process of careful listening and observation, Lake Ridge Community Church ascertained the deepest felt needs of its rapidly growing community and then designed a program to meet those needs.

 Canada's population is composed of more than 200 different ethnicities. Citizenship and Immigration Canada. *Annual Report on the Operation of the Canadian Multiculturalism* Act 2011–2012: Promoting Integration. **www.cic.gc.ca**.

 According to the 2010 "Beyond the Welcome: Churches Responding to the Immigrant Reality in Canada" report, 66 percent of congregations are "always" or "occasionally" providing settlement and relief services for recent immigrants. **www.communitybasedresearch.ca**

HALIFAX,
NOVA SCOTIA

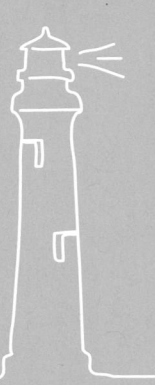

DROWNING IN DEBT
— LIFTED BY FAITH

31. DROWNING IN DEBT — LIFTED BY FAITH

It is Sunday morning at Faith Tabernacle Church in Halifax, Nova Scotia. The cars of worshippers are parked curbside in front of the colourful row houses that line Summit Street, and give Halifax's North End part of its distinctive charm. Some of the houses look like they've been dressed in their own Sunday best in fresh, bright colours with manicured trees and hedges. Others peel and sag. They've seen better days.

This is one of those urban core neighbourhoods that are a mix of the hip and the long-settled.

"Welcome, Church!" is what the young (and yes, very hip) worship leader says as he picks up his guitar and leads a lengthy time of praise. He uses the word church in this way several times, as if he is naming the people who are present—black, white, young, old, rich, poor—as Church.

It feels like a reminder. This is what you are. This is who you are. Faith Tabernacle is trying to figure out "how they are" in the midst of this community that, as Pastor John Cheyne observes, is increasingly in need of financial salvation as well as spiritual. "If people were starving, we would find the bread. If people needed water, we'd give them fresh, clean water," he says. "Here is a real need that is on our doorstep."

The need is to grapple with the ever-rising average Canadian household debt levels—and the fallout damage to the family. "I think it's naïve of the church to worry about some of the social issues we do without even considering the elephant in the room," says Cheyne. "There are some issues we are the best equipped as the Christian community to speak on. The Bible has a lot to say about finances, debt, hard work and so on. For many Canadians in our community here, debt or the threat of debt is overwhelming and putting extraordinary strain on families."

On this Sunday morning, Cheyne preaches a passionate sermon on following God now, and acting in obedience today. In his talk he refers briefly to Mohny Signh, a member of Faith Tabernacle who is a financial advisor trying to create one new way for the Church to help Canadians tidy up their messy finances.

Singh uses a measuring tape to show people how much time they have lived (a lot) and how much life they have left (usually not as much as they thought). Singh's measuring tape is a sober wake-up call for Canadians careening toward retirement. He uses the prop in financial planning workshops he presents in four Nova Scotia churches, including Faith. Singh is clear that this endeavour is both ministry and business, and it is a part of Faith's response to the financial crisis they see more and more often around them.

> I THINK IT'S NAÏVE OF THE CHURCH TO WORRY ABOUT SOME OF THE SOCIAL ISSUES WE DO WITHOUT EVEN CONSIDERING THE ELEPHANT IN THE ROOM.

Singh refers to his plan as a financial GPS, driving you where you want to go: "It is a goal, a plan and a system. It is a unique, lifelong, biblically based financial plan," he says, that sets Christians on the path to tithing, saving and ultimately—if they end up using Singh and any of his advisors for their planning—supporting mission work (Singh donates 70 percent of his profits to overseas work). "We are trying to further the kingdom of God locally and globally by running a profitable business," says

Singh. "When people are empowered, they can give more and have more to give."

Providing the space for Singh to offer these workshops that train people on subjects including budgeting, insurance and investing is just one way Faith is responding to the changing—and that means worsening—financial realities of the community in which they live and worship. The church's response is not complete yet, says Cheyne. He is still on the hunt for the right mix of missional intention and practical program that will help an even wider demographic battle their financial wars.

Cheyne feels a growing sense of urgency to broaden the services Faith offers. "I don't think we could engage with a family without having some regard of other issues they might have, like food, accommodation, finances," says Cheyne. "We as churches are pretty good at doing that in an overseas context: we give money and send a missionary. But mission is at home, it's right on our doorstep, and it has to include that support for people who are suffering under insurmountable debt."

FAITH TABERNACLE
6225 Summit Street, Halifax, NS | Ph. 902.455.1523
www.faithhalifax.org

MORE TO EXPLORE

 Household debt in Canada fluctuates but seems to be remaining around 163 per cent, meaning households owe $1.63 for every dollar of disposable income. Canadians' household debt burden edges higher in second quarter.
www.theglobeandmail.com

 Financial problems are often listed as one of the top life stressors. 'Top 20 Life-Stressors That Can Trigger Anxiety and Sadness'. **blogs.psychcentral.com**

 Approximately 25 percent of Jesus' teachings touched on money and stewardship. **www.christianpf.com**

VANCOUVER, BRITISH COLUMBIA

MINISTRY IN AN UNEXPECTED PLACE

32. MINISTRY IN AN UNEXPECTED PLACE

It is 9:30 on a Wednesday morning at the Washing Wells Laundromat on Commercial Avenue in East Vancouver. The low, continuous hum of large, industrial machines—swishing and spinning, tumbling and drying—has yet to really begin, but the air is thick with the warm, sweet fragrance of yesterday's soap and fabric softener.

People trickle in, carrying soiled laundry in plastic bags, baskets and bins. Linda Obiri-Darko, a middle-aged African-Canadian woman with a broad, friendly smile rushes in to greet the regulars. She usually arrives a few minutes after they do; most of the dozen or so people who typically come here on Wednesday mornings live within walking distance of the laundromat. Obiri-Darko takes a city bus to be here to offer what she believes is valuable ministry to low-income and homeless people in the Grandview-Woodlands neighbourhood.

Everyone has to wash their clothes once in a while. But what is a simple domestic chore for most Canadians isn't so simple for those without washing machines or with limited financial resources. As Obiri-Darko and another volunteer serve coffee and muffins to the assembled group, then hand out loonies and quarters, laundry soap and sheets of fabric softener, it is evident ministry is occurring in this unexpected place.

"Some people haven't had anything to eat for breakfast," Obiri-Darko says. "Some people like to keep to themselves. Some people like to chat with me and tell me how they're doing. I'm there to build relationship, so if people want to come and chat I'm open to that."

Obiri-Darko coordinates the CLEAN (Community Laundry Enterprise Assisting Neighbours) Break program for Grandview Calvary Baptist Church, a large, blue-grey stucco building located a few blocks away from the Washing Wells. Grandview is actually home to two relatively small congregations—one that meets Sunday morning and the other Sunday evening—totaling about 300 people. The church has maintained a presence in this community since 1908. But it hasn't always offered free laundry to people who need it.

Twenty-five years ago, when Tim Dickau first arrived as the new senior pastor at Grandview, the church was very different. Back then the congregation was "50 or 60 people," says Dickau. "Pretty well all seniors. The church had decided to quit."

Today, Grandview is a true parish church: over 60 percent of the congregation lives within the neighbourhood. Many live in proximity to one another and have cultivated a shared life through which they strive to be increasingly hospitable to their community. They've found plenty of ways to do it.

Dickau lists examples: "Housing for refugee claimants. Housing for people dealing with poverty or mental health issues. Social enterprises for people with barriers to employment. An organization that works with trafficked women. A retreat place and place of prayer one block from the church building. An arts program for children, where they learn the stories of the Bible and artistic skills to tell them to the neighbourhood, and to the church. A support group for single mothers." He adds, "So the church has found a number of ways of engaging our community, and particularly those on the margins."

The renewed and diverse ministry began 16 years ago. Dickau was at a neighbourhood meeting of health and social service professionals, when somebody asked what the local churches

> GRANDVIEW IS A TRUE PARISH CHURCH: OVER 60 PERCENT OF THE CONGREGATION LIVES WITHIN THE NEIGHBOURHOOD.

were doing about the increasing numbers of homeless people on Commercial Drive. "They asked me that question because I was the pastor there, and the chair of that group," Dickau says. He wasn't aware of anything being done.

He challenged his congregation with that same question. They responded by developing a free weekly program called Out of the Cold, which provided a meal on Thursday evenings, overnight shelter, and breakfast the next morning. Four years later the church rented a house in the neighbourhood, which they called Crossroads. It became a place to further the relationships that were developing at Out of the Cold, and where the church could help people to connect with other resources.

Crossroads became a home for people who had no home. People could drop in to use the art room, the shower, the kitchen, the computers or the laundry facilities. Five years later, when the facility had to close because the city would not grant the required permit, the church decided on a different approach to addressing the needs of the homeless.

"We said, 'Let's try to connect neighbours with neighbours,'" remembers Dickau. It was in the midst of that effort that the CLEAN Break ministry was born.

"At first I thought it would be overwhelming," admits Obiri-Darko, who says she agreed to coordinate the program with some trepidation. "But it's been really great."

"These people have become friends. I can't walk down the street without meeting someone who says hi. And they've gotten to know each other and become friends with each other. It works both ways."

MORE TO EXPLORE

 When family breaks down and people lose their support network, they can wind up on the street or be left to struggle on their own and on the margins, sometimes for years. Grandview Calvary Baptist Church is reaching out to people who lack family supports.

 We are a country of city-dwellers and urban poverty can be the most persistent kind of poverty. Scoffield, Heather. "Big cities attracting poverty, Statscan data show." *The Globe and Mail*. June 21, 2011. **www.theglobeandmail.com**

 The Vanier Institute of the Family in Ottawa defines "family" as: Any combination of two or more persons who are bound together over time by ties of mutual consent, birth and/or adoption or placement and who, together, assume responsibilities for variant combinations of some of the following:

- Physical maintenance and care of group members
- Addition of new members through procreation or adoption
- Socialization of children
- Social control of members
- Production, consumption, distribution of goods and services
- Affective nurturance – love.

GRANDVIEW CALVARY BAPTIST
1803 East 1st Avenue, Vancouver, BC | Ph. 604.255.1411
www.gcbchurch.ca

33. SMALL CHURCH —BIG TECH IMPACT

It is midday, mid-week in Ajax, Ontario. The sidewalks are mostly new and mostly empty—it looks like a very pretty ghost town. Leafy trees that line the wide streets are not yet as tall as the pretty lampposts that stand in front of the spacious detached homes—the least expensive houses in the Greater Toronto Area, according to a real estate site that trumpets the value of living in this commuter community.

It is this real estate—the carefully planned green spaces and the vast blue of Lake Ontario lapping up one edge of this growing space—that attracts the families that move here, often from Toronto, and often only to get up very early and turn around and go right back into the city for work.

Ajax is suburbia supreme in Southern Ontario.

From 4:15 a.m. onward, trains pull out of the Ajax station, full of commuters making the 45-minute run downtown.

This relentless shifting of people back and forth caught the eye—and ears—of Ryan Sim. Sent to plant a church with The Anglican Church of Canada, Sim spent six months in "missional listening," trying to determine what kind of church would take root in Ajax.

"I was reading demographics, reading everything I could online. I did some online surveys. I drove out here to meet with people," says Sim. "I did chain sampling where I'd start with someone and asked them who else I could talk to."

He included church leaders, of course, assuring them that this plant was for new disciples only, people a bit like him. Sim is 34, married with two children. His demographic is young families, who've never been part of a church or who are long absent, frantically busy, commuting-kinds of people. People with their eyes glued to their smartphones all the way to Union Station.

"I was wondering how we get the Gospel to them where they are, so Jesus can transform their lives, rather than ask them to transform their lives to meet Jesus in the first place," says Sim. "Eighty-seven percent of working age adults commute outside of Ajax to work. People looking at their smartphones provide an opportunity to help them think about big questions in life and offer them help."

And so Redeem the Commute was born. A free app Sim designed specifically for Ajax commuters, Redeem the Commute offers marriage, parenting and a Christianity 101 course—and ongoing invitations to meet up in person eventually.

A clip opens with a high-blood-pressure-inducing shot of a packed 401 highway and trains charging out of the station. Sim perches beside playground equipment introducing the parenting course: "I'm a father living in Ajax starting a new church for busy commuting families. This parenting course is our gift to you..." What follows are world-famous Alpha courses edited into 10-minute clips: bite-sized doses of wisdom and challenge for weary parents sitting on trains.

Always there is a nudge to talk with someone else, to form a group, to connect with Sim in person. But that's where things did not go quite as planned.

While the app was picked up by a number of Ajax commuters, it may be that these folks are busier than even Sim could imagine. He's still sifting through the reasons why, two years in, the online community that Sim helped create has not translated into bodies in a room worshipping together, or even doing a course in person.

That was the plan. Find them online. Fill a need. Connect in person.

"It either totally confirms our theory that people around here are just way too busy, no matter how convenient we make it, or maybe it's just not something people need. They are parenting young kids and maybe this doesn't answer their questions," says Sim. "I haven't quite landed on it yet. I still have more questions. We just keep trying new things. We're trying to try the right things. Some work and some don't."

> **WE'RE TRYING TO TRY THE RIGHT THINGS. SOME WORK AND SOME DON'T.**

The app worked for Karen Malone, a 50-something scuba shop manager from nearby Oshawa. She was already attending church but found a traditional Sunday service unhelpful. "I was looking for answers and didn't get them in a Sunday service that was so regimented," says Malone. "Ryan has these online courses and study things, so I get more out of all that interaction than I do from going once a week on Sunday. The organized churches, their schedules are so rigid and limited—this gives you the option to explore that path on your own, on the GO train or at home on your computer. Those who don't live inside the typical routine need something else. It gives you that."

Malone was one of the few who made the shift from online consumer of Christianity 101 to an in-person attendee at the same course offered by Sim in a local church. She says her faith has grown. But the vast majority of the growing group of Redeem the Commute users (the app has been downloaded on 1300 devices at last count) have not moved from online to in-person.

Even as Sim has been building Redeem the Commute, supplying an ongoing stream of the Daily Challenge—where, in addition to the courses, users are offered a "new idea," some Bible teaching, reflection and then action—he has been doing ministry the old-fashioned way, too. Hanging out in coffee shops, making friends with neighbours, listening. Hosting Christianity 101 in person for people like Karen. There's even been one baptism of a single mom, held at the Carruthers Marsh Pavilion.

"Of all the choices in front of us about how to plant a church, we didn't do any of the easy things," reflects Sim. "We've intentionally moved to a community full of commuters. We've made it as difficult as possible. Every church planter will tell you that they have hard soil. That's our hard soil."

The whole world is hard soil these days, he acknowledges.

So, there is another plan being created from yet more listening. A Sunday morning gathering designed especially for "busy parents whose kids are in daycare all week. They think it's a shame to stick them in Sunday School. The idea is to develop a church that families will attend together," says Sim. "I've been here long enough [two years], we have a great communication platform. We have enough missional listening and enough presence in the community to do that and think it might work."

It is a very light service, what a die-hard Anglican might find a bit casual.

Sim sits at a picnic table in an Ajax park, soccer balls careening through the air from a pick-up game gone wild nearby. "This is the kind of place you want to plant a church," he says.

"You want to see new disciples made, as tough a nut as it is to crack. We have so many ways to plant a church that attracts Christians. I think we have the opportunity to try something different. To slow it down a bit and ask how we can make new disciples."

Sim says there is a tension, inherent in any church plant, maybe especially in this day and age, and in this place: slow down so people can hear about Jesus, but speed up so they can do it before your funding runs out. "You're always fighting those two tensions: slow down, speed up. You have to find the right pace."

REDEEMER CHURCH
c/o 300 Williamson Drive E, Ajax, ON | Ph. 289.624.4209
www.redeemerajax.ca

MORE TO EXPLORE

 Ryan Sim's innovative app ministers to people right where they are, literally.

 On average, Canadians have 25 apps on their phones.
www.catalyst.ca

 15.4 million Canadians commute to work, according to the 2011 National Household Survey (Census Canada).

 Canadians spend an average of 45.6 hours online each month (Canadian Internet Registration Authority, 2013).

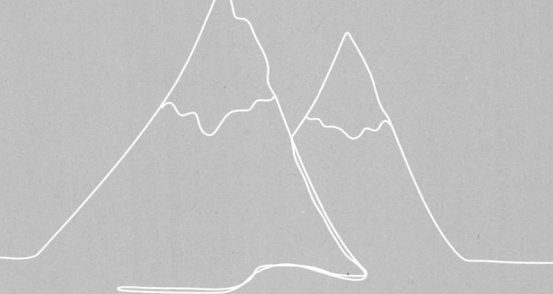

MEDICINE HAT, ALBERTA

BENEVOLENCE WITHOUT BRANDING

34. BENEVOLENCE WITHOUT BRANDING

It's not every church that can tell of owning three large cargo containers and two semi-trailers. But then, it's not every church that needs them.

Hillcrest Evangelical Missionary Church in Medicine Hat, Alberta does. The trailers and containers are visible evidence of a congregation determined to live its declared mission: "Ministering God's love to a hurting world."

One of the ways Hillcrest works out that mission is by addressing some of the most pressing, practical needs in their community—needs resulting from financial and family woes. In a city with a population of just over 70,000 people, where fully one-third of income earners do not earn a living wage, that's a tall order. But they don't do it alone. The wind beneath this church's wings is the working partnership they've developed with multiple community organizations.

The Hillcrest website states that the congregation believes in community involvement. "Rather than come up with a new initiative we see the value in partnering with what is already going on in our city," it reads.

Situated directly on the Trans-Canada Highway, one of the realities going on in this city is that women from across the country—who are fleeing abusive relationships—frequently find their way to the safety and relative obscurity of The Medicine Hat Women's Shelter Society. The Society supports women and children who have experienced family violence by providing them with safe shelter, education and access to community resources.

Through their furniture ministry, Hillcrest Church redistributes literal tonnes of community resources every year. It all began 12 years ago when a former church staffer started scanning classified ads for used washers and dryers, picking them up and delivering them to people in need. Hillcrest no longer deals in large appliances, but the church collects donations of gently used beds, couches, tables and chairs, bedding, dishes, towels and small appliances, and then drops them off to clients of several community organizations, including the women's shelter.

It is a massive undertaking, one that requires not only the storage and transportation options provided by the aforementioned cargo containers and semi-trailers, but also a host of volunteers committed to picking up, sorting through and dropping off donations. Every week of the year. Hillcrest delivers furniture and household goods to some 600 individuals annually, helping an average of 140 mostly single-parent, single-income families get back on their feet in the wake of often appalling life experiences.

"As long as we've got a referral," says Clinton Cairns, outreach pastor at Hillcrest, "we've done stuff for Alberta Human Services, the Canadian Mental Health Association, Medicine Hat Community Housing, Alberta Health Services, an agency in town that helps new immigrants, and the women's shelter."

Rose O'Donnell is assistant director at the women's shelter. She speaks enthusiastically about the difference the church makes in the lives of their clients. When the women first arrive, she says, "Sometimes all they have is the clothes on their backs. They don't have furniture. They don't have anything." But Hillcrest Church, she says, "just keeps coming through for us. It's a great partnership."

"We had a...lady come in fleeing her adult child who was abusing her," she remembers. The shelter helped the woman locate a seniors' apartment. And then, "We got furniture from Hillcrest. She now has a job walking dogs. She's involved with the Seniors' Centre, and all because they were able to get her restarted. I mean, she was 65 and she had nothing until they were able to give it to her."

The church's furniture ministry is not their only community care initiative. A Benevolent Fund assists people in financial need by providing one-time support—ranging from $100 to $2,500—to cover everything from emergency rent payments to utility bills. And, in partnership with the Canadian Mental Health Association, the church hosts monthly budgeting-for-beginners workshops.

In partnership with the local food bank, Hillcrest also runs a lunch program for children in the community that makes and distributes 380 school lunches every weekday to 22 schools throughout the school year. Cairns personally drives a daily route to deliver lunches to seven elementary schools.

An employee of the Medicine Hat Food Bank, Karrey Crooks coordinates the Brown Bag Lunch Program. She says the free lunches represent "a huge burden lifted" from the families that need that kind of assistance. She has the thank you cards, letters from parents, school administrators and children to prove it.

"Many families struggle to pay their rent, mortgage, utilities, car payments, et cetera," says Crooks. "Sometimes there's just more month than pay cheque. It puts their mind at ease that every day their child is receiving a nutritious lunch, which also helps with the growing grocery budget."

> WE'RE WANTING TO BE THAT LINK WITH THE COMMUNITY. WE DON'T WANT TO START NEW PROGRAMS JUST SO WE CAN HAVE OUR CHURCH NAME ON THEM.

Hillcrest Church has been "absolutely fundamental" to the program, she says. "Without their commercial kitchen, and them paying all the utilities, et cetera to go along with the running of it, we would not be able to do this."

Cairns doesn't worry about the fact that people in the community may not even realize it is Hillcrest behind the response to so many fundamental needs. "We're wanting to be that link with the community," he explains. "We don't want to start new programs just so we can have our church name on them.

"My philosophy is people don't really care at the end of the day about the name [behind the good deeds]. I think it speaks a lot louder to our community when we can partner with our community in what they're already doing instead of trying to boost our own brand. There's enough branding out there. We don't need to do more of our own."

HILLCREST EVANGELICAL MISSIONARY CHURCH
3785 13th Avenue SE, Medicine Hat, AB | Ph. 403.526.4010
www.hillcrestchurch.net

SHIFTING STATS

MORE TO EXPLORE

 In 1961, more than nine out of 10 (92 percent) Canadian census families contained a married couple. Fifty years later, by 2011, fewer than seven out of 10 did (67 percent). Meanwhile, the number of lone-parent families in Canada almost doubled over the same 50-year period. Statistics Canada. "Census in Brief: Fifty Years of Families in Canada: 1961–2011." **www12.statcan.gc.ca**

 The median net worth of lone-parent families headed by a female in Canada is just $14,000—the lowest of any family type in the country. Vanier Institute of the Family. "Money and the Canadian Family." Transition. (Winter 2002-2003) Vol. 32, No. 4. **www.vanierinstitute.ca**

 Vital Signs Canada reports that the median income in Medicine Hat has risen by 10.3 percent since 2008, yet 10 percent of the population still lives below the Low Income Measure (LIM). Over 60 percent of those are women. www.vitalsignscanada.ca

**WINNIPEG,
MANITOBA**

WELCOMING DIVERSITY IN WINNIPEG

35. WELCOMING DIVERSITY IN WINNIPEG

"Dëërïjööt." That is one way of saying hello in Dha-Anywaa, the language of the Anyuak, one of the ethnic communities from Ethiopia that is slowly but surely sliding into pews in Lutheran Church-Canada churches. Particularly in Winnipeg.

Saying hello—in English will do—is the first simple step that Canadian churches need to take to welcome immigrants into their midst, says Oboya Ochalla, who landed in Winnipeg when he arrived in Canada in 2003.

"Canadian people, they are nice people, they are good people," says Ochalla "It's good for them if they can open their hand and open their church for the immigrant. Be nice. Be truthful. Be faithful." When Ochalla arrived in Canada, he knew no one. "But I do pray always that God can show me somewhere like a church where I can go, and nice people, where I can live."

In Ethiopia, Ochalla was a teacher. Here he works as a security guard, with another part-time job on the side to support his family. He is also working through the Pastors with Alternate Training program (PAT) of the Lutheran Church-Canada (LCC). Established in 2002, PAT prepares pastors for ministry within specific cultural groups, to help LCC meet the changing face of Canada's population.

"My background is that I'm a Christian," explains Ochalla. "Since I came to Canada I had been looking for a church I could go to. There are so many churches. I prefer to go to the Lutheran Church."

He loves the liturgy: the "Take, eat, this is my body," poetry of the prayer of institution in the communion service; the cadence of the Agnus Dei where worshippers are reminded of the sacrificial Lamb; and the post-Communion canticle where God is praised for his grace and mercy. The rich, melodic service reminds him of home.

Ochalla leads an Anyuak service at Immanuel Lutheran Church on King Edward Street every Sunday at noon, just after the regular morning service in English, which he attends as well.

Rev. Dr. Richard Beinert is Immanuel's pastor, and a champion for Winnipeg's Christian immigrant population. He says members of the Anyuak community began to trickle into his church one Christmas a few years ago. In the new world of Winnipeg—with their first, terrible winter upon them—the familiar rhythm and cadence of the Lutheran church, which has had missionary roots in Ethiopia's soil since the late 1800s, warmed their hearts.

The trickle widened to a stream, until it was clear there were enough people with a desire and need for a service in their "heart language." That's where Ochalla and his PAT training enter the sanctuary.

Immanuel, Beinert says, is becoming a "global community. We are a mid-sized congregation. The progress we see with these inroads God has given us in Winnipeg—it's amazing how far the ripples go."

Church potlucks now feature African fare alongside perogies. Choirs from the two services blend together at special occasions, creating one lovely and holy sound.

Understanding, though, has required a long drive down a two-way street—complete with potholes and the occasional detour.

SHIFTING STATS

> **WE FEEL LIKE WE ARE IN OUR HOME WHEN WE ARE WELCOMED BY THE PEOPLE.**

Winnipeg's church community needed to understand that even Africans from the same nation—Ethiopia—can come from very different ethnic, language and religious groups. Beinert's one congregation alone reached out to two very different groups of Ethiopians, for example: the Oromo and the Anyuak.

And new Canadians came to see that a Lutheran—or any other Church—stance on an issue in Ethiopia may be as different in Canada as a summer night in Addis Ababa is to a winter morning in Winnipeg. Theology can divide like an ocean between continents.

"New Canadians may come to a church and say 'What is going on?'" says Beinert. "The shift to allowing same sex marriage within liberal communities [in Canada] has proven to be difficult for the immigrant community. They will come to Canada and run into this dynamic," he explains. "The Oromo were not, at first, aware of the difference. They discovered their values were more associated with our Church," as opposed to other Lutheran expressions that exist in Canada.

As for the learning curve for Canadians: "It's the North American thing," says Beinert, "where we think all Africans are the same. There are very different cultural identities across Africa and even within countries. Some of it has to do with their cultural experience over the past century, some of it has to do with organizational things within their community."

The Anyuak, for example, consider themselves happily part of Immanuel while the Oromo chose to worship in their own building with their congregation, initially under the oversight of Beinert.

Taking time to get to know the communities is the only way to really understand, says Beinert.

"Welcome them. Let them know that your church can be their home. I'd even go stronger than that and say: this is your church home. Work on that."

And don't be afraid. Luther himself has some wisdom to share on this, according to Beinert. "Luther had a wonderful phrase: sin boldly," he says. "That doesn't mean that we are to go out and sin intentionally, but acknowledging that we are going to make mistakes along the way—just keep on moving ahead with your eyes on the cross. It's like the old story about the centipede: after someone asked him how he kept track of each of his legs while walking, the moment he stopped to think about it, he found that he couldn't walk anymore. Sometimes we overthink our outreach and ministry."

And remember, Dëërijööt is one way to say hello in Dha-Anywaa. "We feel like we are in our home," says Ochalla, "when we are welcomed by the people."

IMMANUEL LUTHERAN CHURCH
2528 King Edward Street, Winnipeg, MB | Ph. 204.632.6911
www.mts.net/~IMLC/home

MORE TO EXPLORE

 The PAT program of the Lutheran Church-Canada was created to respond to the increase in Canada's ethnic diversity and to address the challenges to churches to provide pastoral ministry to immigrant populations in their own language and context.

 Canada has a higher percentage of foreign-born citizens than any other G8 country, according to CanadianImmigrant.ca.

 Statistics Canada reports more than 200 languages were noted in the 2011 Census. **www12.statcan.gc.ca**

MIDDLETON, NOVA SCOTIA

SINGLE PARENTS:
BUILDING BRIDGES

36. SINGLE PARENTS: BUILDING BRIDGES

Middleton, Nova Scotia, is a small town in the heart of the beautiful Annapolis Valley. The town, popular with tourists, is home to one of only three rare water clocks in North America, as well as the quaint Memory Lane Railway Museum and a startlingly high percentage of families led by single parents (20.8 percent compared to a provincial total several points lower).

Deb Cadden, director of the single parent program at Emmanuel Congregational Christian Church, doesn't know exactly why there are so many single-parent families in her town. But she knew her church had to do something to help this part of the population especially vulnerable to the tough economic times that have rocked this valley for several years now. Call centres that used to be steady, go-to employers have moved on. When IKEA cancelled its contract with a furniture factory, 200 more people lost their jobs.

"Rural life is not like it was," says Cadden. "People used to earn their livings off the land and they are not doing it now." People also aren't getting married like they used to, and the vast majority of single parent families are led by young women struggling to make it on their own, with little support. "Single parents are today's widows and orphans," says Deb.

Enter Deb and her team (currently 24 volunteers strong) with Just Me and the Kids, a made-in-Canada, tried-and-true ministry resource for churches to help single parents in their communities. The program, which is still available online (even though the ministry behind it is no longer in existence), is built around a mid-week meal served up for the parents and children, who then head off to different rooms for a children's program and a parents' support group. The single moms (for that is mostly who comes) discuss their weeks, their feelings and their challenges in their discussion group.

Discussing your feelings is all well and good, of course, but Deb and her team quickly detected that the parents coming out wanted and needed more than that. "The program we were using is really aimed at people who have lost a spouse through death or divorce," explains Deb. "In the first group we did, the parents had been married, but in our second group not one of them had been married. They were single parents in today's modern culture."

The Emmanuel team began to nip and tuck the program, making it fit the needs they saw before them. That meant getting very, very practical. "We have done a cooking day. We've had a retired judge come in to discuss wills and court processes for people going through court battles," she says. "This year we will have workshops on childcare and handling children.

"One of the biggest needs we've seen," says Deb, "is budgeting and learning how to handle your finances. Some of the younger girls who have never been married and come in with a baby on their hip, their parents have thrown them out. They have no idea how to handle money." Financial training and budgeting will be part of the program from here on.

The group is slowly building (averaging five new families every time Emmanuel offers it, with most of the veterans returning, and often leading subsequent sessions.) Word is also getting out that the church where it is offered is not trying to mess up your life. "Church is a very scary place for some people," says Deb. "People don't know. Once they've been there they realize we are not these total religious fanatics that are going to convert them no matter what."

Jamie Earnshaw, 29, is a single mom to two young children. She overcame her initial reluctance and attended Emmanuel's single parent program. "I thought the church was a negative place. I thought it was a bunch of rules I had to follow and I couldn't be myself," she says. Once in though, she was quickly hooked. "They offered support and just advice on where to go, what to do. It really, for me, turned into a small family," says Jamie. "I got so close with everyone there, with my fellow classmates. It was good to connect with others, to give advice and to take advice."

> **SINGLE PARENTS ARE TODAY'S WIDOWS AND ORPHANS.**

She also got close to God, realizing for the first time how deeply loved she was. "It still takes my breath away when I think that I almost didn't go to this group. A lot of people are afraid—they think someone is going to slap them in the face with the Bible." What she discovered instead was people just wanting to help. "Knowing that God will still love you and you have someone in your corner, this program offers it and offers a place where you can go and be accepted, and your kids can be accepted."

For churches looking for ways to get into the community and reach people, Jamie advises they look at the single-parent families in the community. "I think that the people who are in need most are the ones who are by themselves; they are often single parents," she says. "When you get support, it is empowering. If every church had one of these programs, the church community would grow." And the single parents, says Jamie, wouldn't feel so single after all.

> "As a family therapist, I have seen too often the effects on mothers of loneliness and poverty. Nourishing these mothers spiritually and practically will strengthen their bonds of attachment and care for the developing lives of their children, and will lift the burden of shame and isolation from their shoulders."
>
> – **Diane Marshall**,
> Registered Marriage and Family Therapist,
> Institute of Family Living

EMMANUEL CONGREGATIONAL CHRISTIAN CHURCH
37 Gates Avenue, Middleton, NS | Ph. 902.825.1777
www.emmanuelchurch.ca

MORE TO EXPLORE

 Lone-parent families made up 16.3% of all census families in 2011. *Fifty Years of Families in Canada: 1961 to 2011.* **www12.statcan.gc.ca**

 The rate of poverty among lone-parent families is four times as high as two-parent families.

 Statistics Canada offers a search-by-community option where you can find out the statistical breakdown of demographics in towns and cities across Canada. **www.statcan.gc.ca**

LLOYDMINSTER, SASKATCHEWAN

HOW "CHRISTIAN" BECAME MORE THAN JUST A NAME

37. HOW "CHRISTIAN" BECAME MORE THAN JUST A NAME

With dark brown, shoulder-length hair, a porcelain-doll complexion and a dimpled smile, eighteen-year-old Cassandra Christian suits her name: she looks every inch the wholesome young adult she is. In fact, "Christian" describes both her surname and her faith. But it wasn't always so. A few short years ago, Christian admits she was a "Christian" in name only.

"I didn't really have my own faith," she says, when asked what she was like before her youth group changed. Three years ago, the group at First Baptist Church of Lloydminster (FBCOL), Saskatchewan, morphed from an attractional model—focusing on Friday night fun and games—to something quite different. "My faith was my mom's faith," Christian adds. "I just went to church because my mom took me there." She wasn't alone.

While Statistics Canada data indicates a majority of residents in Lloydminster consider themselves Christian, Darren Bute, youth pastor at FBCOL says the evidence would indicate otherwise. "We're a big oil town, so employment and incomes are high," he says. "The drug culture is quite prevalent here. Sports are huge. Hockey is a major influence in this town. There are a high number of people involved in the party scene, because there's such a huge amount of disposable income."

Given that Christianity is always influenced by its surrounding culture, a party environment outside the church might be expected to show up in some way inside the church, particularly among the youth. But Bute says several years ago he sensed a growing dissatisfaction with FBCOL's youth ministry. In spite of the fun and games, it wasn't going well. "We were seeing kids dropping out after grades 10, 11, 12, and not coming back to church. I felt like I was being looked at more as an event planner or entertainer than a youth pastor.

"I came to the conclusion I didn't want to do that anymore."

What he and his leadership team agreed they did want was to see young adults come out of the youth program as thriving, growing, committed disciples. Next, Bute and his team asked themselves what disciples are like, and what disciples do. They created a list. "Games wasn't on our list," says Bute, "so we got rid of them."

The team determined that going forward their youth ministry would be a place where they would do the things disciples do. That list included building compassionate community and providing opportunities for worship, spiritual growth and service.

In September 2011, weekly youth meetings at FBCOL moved from Fridays to Sunday evenings. They began with a hot meal and were followed by a time of music, informal teaching and testimonies. Sunday School was scrapped, leaving youth free to serve on Sunday mornings. Mid-week small groups were instituted for Bible study and prayer.

The fallout was immediate. "As soon as we made the switch, we lost about half our youth group," Bute remembers. "We went from averaging 60 kids a night to about 25."

Executive pastor Doug Baynton remembers the time as "an adjustment," but says they knew there was no turning back. "It was a pretty big deviation from traditional youth ministry, but when you make those types of decisions, you're 'in for a penny, in for a pound.' We knew this wasn't something we would be reversing course on." And they didn't. But there was pushback, particularly from the young people.

> I FELT LIKE I WAS BEING LOOKED AT MORE AS AN EVENT PLANNER OR ENTERTAINER THAN A YOUTH PASTOR. I CAME TO THE CONCLUSION I DIDN'T WANT TO DO THAT ANYMORE.

"I hated it," says Christian. But slowly, her attitude started to change. "It was a gradual thing," she remembers. "I started growing deeper in my faith. I started wanting to learn more." And once again, she wasn't alone.

By the end of the first ministry season, the numbers had returned to almost previous levels, but with a slightly different group of young people. By the end of the second season, numbers surpassed those before the change. But growth has not only been quantitative, it's been about quality. Where youth once had an expectation of being served and entertained, now they serve—willingly—in everything from children's ministry and worship teams to folding bulletins. They're giving financially and of their time. Senior high youth assist adults in leading junior high small groups, and act as mentors. Many have participated in short-term mission trips. And they're sticking around after they graduate.

"What we're seeing is spiritual growth," says Baynton. "They're not just kids that are here for the sake of events. They're serious about their faith, and they're growing in their faith, and they're trying to expand their faith both personally and interpersonally to others as well. We're seeing them get involved in sharing their faith, and in missions—both locally and internationally. And they're going for the right reasons. They're motivated differently than they have been in the past."

Christian has officially graduated from youth group, but she's continuing on as a small group leader for younger girls. It's a task she relishes, because it's a group she cares for deeply. "Their faith is a lot more solid than mine ever was at that age," she says. "Because they're being fed. Kids know now that that's what's going to happen at youth. It's all focused on our relationship with Christ."

As for Bute, he says he used to regularly get messages from youth asking "What are we doing this week?" But even that's changed. "I don't get those texts or phone calls anymore," he says.

"They know what we're doing. We're going to connect with Jesus."

> "In the brokenness of our world, we first 'compare' and then out of that comparison, we are moved to compassion. Jesus, when he walked on the earth, was moved with compassion first. To teach our students how to be people of compassion is the true mark of a Jesus' style evangelism."
>
> **– Matt Wilks**,
> Team Leader, Canadian Youth Worker

FIRST BAPTIST CHURCH LLOYDMINSTER
3915 47 Avenue, Lloydminster, SK | Ph. 306-825-2451
www.fbclloyd.ca

MORE TO EXPLORE

Since 1984, the percentage of teens who call themselves "Christian" has been almost cut in half, while the numbers who call themselves "atheist" has grown to 16 percent, up from just 6 percent in the mid-1980s. Lunau, Kate. "Youth Survey: Teens lose faith in droves." *Maclean's*, April 7, 2009. **www2.macleans.ca**

According to the *Hemorrhaging Faith* study:

- "Youth and young adults who are not engaged in the church have not experienced a sense of belonging and community in their church contexts."

- "Young adults are more likely to stay engaged in the church if they are directly involved in the missional activities of the church. "'Hemorrhaging Faith: Why and When Canadian Young Adults are Leaving, Staying and Returning to Church'. Toronto: EFC Youth and Young Adult Ministry Roundtable, 2013. **www.tgcfcanada.org/hemorrhagingfaith**

38. HARVESTING FRUIT AND FRIENDSHIP

Drive along the Queen Elizabeth Way (QEW) from Toronto to Hamilton to the Niagara Peninsula and you travel from the core of Ontario's largest commercial and industrial centres into the heart of fruit and wine country.

It is in the shadow of the Niagara Escarpment that some of the province's most fertile farmland lies. Acre upon acre of orchards and vineyards, all beautifully groomed and carefully tended, provide testimony to the hidden hands that work long hours planting and pruning, thinning and harvesting.

But leave the highway to drive some of the backcountry avenues of the Niagara Greenbelt and evidence of those hidden hands may become more visible. Dark-skinned men riding bicycles or walking single file along roadsides to and from unknown destinations hint at the truth: it is thousands of seasonal agricultural workers from places like Mexico, Jamaica, and Trinidad and Tobago who are helping to cultivate the farms that provide the luscious peaches, cherries, raspberries and other produce to countless Canadian grocery stores throughout the summer season.

"There are hundreds and hundreds of men here who are almost invisible," says Tim Arnold, outreach pastor at Southridge Community Church in Vineland, Ontario. Behind the wheel of his car—en route to visit a few of them—he adds, "More than anything, what these guys need are friends."

For this day's visit Arnold is joined, as he often is, by a feisty, 79-year-old grey-haired woman named Mary Ann Schlabach. The migrant workers know her as "Sister Mary Ann."

"Since '66, I've been involved in the guys' lives," she says.

It was in 1966 that the Canadian government established the Seasonal Agricultural Workers Program (SAWP) as a way of bringing Jamaican men to Canada to help make up for a shortage of local farm workers. "The guys" as Schlabach refers to them, have been coming ever since.

Today, close to 30,000 farm workers migrate to Canada for up to eight months of each year through SAWP. They leave behind wives and children in their native lands to live and work in Canada throughout the growing season. They stay in trailers, barns and modest houses, and are paid by the hour, earning only minimum wage. They work hard for little because earning minimum wage far from home is better than being unemployed at home.

Back in '66, "my husband and I owned a little grocery store," Schlabach says. "And these men would come and do their shopping. We would carry their accounts for them. To this day they're grateful for that. It showed that we loved them and trusted them. We started having them in our home, and taking them to church if they wanted to go."

The friendship ministry that Schlabach and a handful of others cultivated amongst the Caribbean workers has endured for decades. But a few years ago Schlabach recognized she wasn't getting any younger, and that the ministry needed to grow. She prayed for helpers.

At about the same time, Southridge's Vineland congregation (a multi-site church with two other congregations located in the nearby cities of St. Catharines and Welland) prayed for outreach opportunities.

"The goal of our outreach is that we would reach out to the most marginalized group in the neighbourhood," says Arnold. "And migrant workers certainly would be that. We just didn't

> THERE ARE HUNDREDS AND HUNDREDS OF MEN HERE WHO ARE ALMOST INVISIBLE. MORE THAN ANYTHING, WHAT THESE GUYS NEED ARE FRIENDS.

know what that would look like. It was very quick that I got connected with Sister Mary Ann. And that's what started all this."

"All this" is a thriving, two-year-old ministry Southridge calls the "Caribbean Workers Program" (CWP). Involving 170 adult members out of a congregation of 300, the program is the Vineland church's main outreach focus. CWP addresses the isolation and lack of community that migrant workers struggle with during their time in Canada. CWP works in teams, each one connected with a different farm. Teams make regular visits to the workers to deliver welcome kits to newcomers (consisting of toiletries, towels, hats and gloves), build relationships, provide friendship and drive the workers to appointments when needed.

Church volunteers fix used bikes to sell to workers at affordable prices, and organize and host monthly social events such as domino tournaments, bowling nights, BBQs, cricket matches and Niagara Falls excursions. They also pray for the program and for special prayer requests from the men.

In partnership with other area churches, Southridge hosts Sunday evening Jamaican worship services each spring that attract an average of 60 to 70 men. They come, attracted by the promise of a visiting Jamaican preacher, and the opportunity to sing songs and hymns, and to worship in a way that reminds them of home.

*

Mark Smikle, 41, is the first friend Arnold and Schlabach visit on this day. He greets the two with hugs and small talk. But when asked about work, he shakes his head. Work has been slow. When the weather is good, Smikle willingly works seven days a week, 12 to 14 hours a day. But when the weather is bad—and it's been bad lately—there is no work, and no pay.

Smikle has been coming to work on Canadian farms from Jamaica for 16 years. With a wife and three daughters back home, he describes his long distance family life as "a difficult challenge," but says the opportunity to earn income here "helps to build the family. It helps to give them a better education."

Education is not free in much of the Caribbean, and Smikle wants to ensure a better life for his children. They're well on their way to attaining it. Smikle proudly relates that his eldest daughter is in university. His middle child is achieving good grades in high school, even as she represents her country internationally in track and field, and his youngest daughter, in primary school, is also working hard.

Smikle gestures to Arnold and Schlabach. "These people are like part of my family," he says softly, in his heavily accented English. "It means a lot to me and to the other guys. They are here for us. We are away from our family, but we can call on them any time."

> "Rural and small town churches have often been the greatest per capita givers to global mission, while missing the invisible migrant workers in their own communities and back roads. Thanks to Sister Mary Ann and Southridge/Vineland for extending the heart and hands of Jesus to these—'just down the road.'"
>
> – **Dan Sheffield**,
> Director, Global and Intercultural Ministries,
> The Free Methodist Church in Canada

SOUTHRIDGE COMMUNITY CHURCH
201 Glenridge Avenue, St. Catharines, ON | Ph. 905.682.9901
www.southridge.cc

*

Arnold pauses to reflect when asked the difference that building friendships with the migrant workers has made in the lives of the people of Southridge Vineland. "They have allowed us to grow in humility," he says finally, "just realizing that there are people in our community that we can so easily not see. I hear from people all the time that these men used to be invisible to them. Now they can't go anywhere without seeing them.

"And certainly, you grow in gratitude for the life you lead. Take Mark, for example. He's a harder worker, he's a smarter man, he's probably a better Christian than me. I just happen to have been born here. And as a result, the opportunities that I've had have allowed me to have a very different life. And you realize that at a whole new level."

MORE TO EXPLORE

The number of migrant workers in Canada has increased by 70% in the last five years. Increase in Temporary Foreign Worker numbers. **www.ccrweb.ca**

Canada has been shifting towards a reliance on migrant labour. In 2008, for the first time, the number of temporary foreign workers in Canada exceeded the total number of permanent residents admitted in the same year.

Migrant workers are especially vulnerable to exploitation and abuse because of their lack of status, their isolation and their lack of access to information on their rights, and because the Canadian and most provincial governments don't ensure monitoring of their workplaces.
www.ccrweb.ca/en/migrant-workers

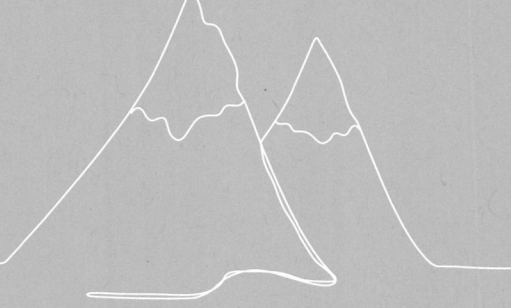

CALGARY, ALBERTA

ADOPTIVE AND FOSTER
FAMILIES FINDING HOPE

39. ADOPTIVE AND FOSTER FAMILIES FINDING HOPE

Helen Schirok, with her blonde hair and green eyes, does not look like she is related to the rambunctious little Chinese boy with the winsome smile who's racing around across the room. But when she calls out to him to be careful, her Australian accent reveals a mother's concern.

"We picked Jensen up from China when he was 13-and-half months-old," she explains. "He was abandoned at four months old. He was found in the street, close to a hospital, with pneumonia and two large holes in his heart."

Now at three-and-a-half and with those holes long since repaired, Jensen is thriving in every way. So is Schirok, thanks in no small part, she says, to the Adoption and Foster Care Ministry at Calgary's First Alliance Church.

It is a ministry that encompasses the monthly playgroup (to which Schirok and her son have come this day to socialize with other adoptive and fostering families) and the aptly named "Empowered to Connect Parent Training," a nine-week course that equips families to understand the unique blessings and challenges associated with rearing non-biological children.

Schirok describes the training she received through Empowered to Connect as "life changing. It gave a lot of insight into the children who'd been affected by trauma." The relational and prayer support she and her husband gained also proved to be invaluable, readying them, Schirok says, for the dramatic life change they would experience when Jensen became their son. Once he did, the playgroup became a safe place for Jensen to play with other adopted children, and a welcome respite for Schirok. She quickly felt comfortable sharing the triumphs and trials of being a newly adoptive parent in an environment with other parents who "all connect with the same story."

"You just totally understand one another," Schirok says. "You don't have to explain."

Launched in 2011, the Adoption and Foster Care Ministry takes its Biblical support from the idea of defending the cause of orphans, as expressed in Isaiah 1:17, but organizers add that it's really all about bringing hope and friendship to families.

"There's a lot of brokenness that's part of adoption," says Colleen Derksen, who shares leadership responsibilities for the ministry with her husband Brian, and another couple, Angela and Brian Hargreaves.

"Adoption always comes from loss. A family unit has been broken in some way. So there's loss and grief from the get-go. Some children sail through that with great resilience, others do not—regardless of when they're adopted."

Derksen knows those realities first hand. She and her husband adopted three biological siblings out of Alberta's foster care system. "It's been intense," she says.

The Hargreaves journey was different. "We had one biological son...and then we adopted a little girl," says Angela. "And our quiver is now full," she says, with a light laugh other parents recognize as code that means that some days the quiver feels very full indeed.

Together the Derksens and the Hargreaves make a passionate team that cares deeply about the more than 60 families they've connected with and served since launching the ministry. They

> THIS IS A PLACE THEY CAN COME TO WHERE THEY CAN BE VULNERABLE, WHERE THEY FEEL UNDERSTOOD, WHERE THEIR KIDS ARE ACCEPTED...

say the primary value offered by both the playgroup and the training courses is that people feel less isolated as a result of the support they receive.

"One common theme we've heard from families is that, when they are facing challenges, they can feel very alone," says Derksen. "The church might not be a place they feel they can go to, because they don't have it all together. They feel like their family is falling apart. But this is a place they can come to where they can be vulnerable, where they feel understood, where their kids are accepted and where they get to have that sense of community."

Both women also speak of the support the church has thrown behind the initiative.

As the ministry has connected with increasing numbers of adoptive and foster families, Derksen and Hargreaves have been asked to contribute to the training of children's ministry leaders, so that those leaders can respond to the unique challenges presented by adopted and foster children with awareness and compassion.

"It's a great privilege to adopt children," says Derksen. "But it's also a huge responsibility in terms of how we love them and communicate a sense of their incredible preciousness and worth."

> "The journey of foster care is incredibly gratifying, but it is extremely challenging. Like any challenge in life, the load is more bearable when a supportive community comes alongside to pray for and be a source of encouragement. It is a journey that would be difficult to travel alone."
>
> **– Hank de Jong**,
> Foster Parent, Executive Director,
> EduDeo Ministries

FIRST ALLIANCE CHURCH
12345 40 Street SE, Calgary, AB | Ph. 403.252.7572
www.faccalgary.com

SHIFTING STATS

MORE TO EXPLORE

 While the Adoption and Foster Care Ministry at First Alliance Church in Calgary has a strong, committed leadership team in place, both the impact of the initiative—and the leaders themselves—have been strengthened by the support of the pastoral team and of the broader church community.

 The Evangelical Fellowship of Canada has created Adoption Sunday to generate a greater national awareness of adoption and fostering, and to provide free downloadable resources for church use. **www.adoptionsunday.com**

 Of the more than 78,000 children in Canada's child welfare system, approximately 30,000 are legally eligible for adoption. Adoption Council of Canada.
www.adoption.ca/myths-and-realities

 Approximately one in five Canadians is touched by adoption. They are either adopted themselves, have an adopted sibling or family member, are adoptive parents, birth parents or birth relatives. Today, that means almost seven million Canadians are affected by adoption. Adoption Council of Canada.
www.adoption.ca/myths-and-realities

CRASHING THE TIME CRUNCH

40. CRASHING THE TIME CRUNCH

For 131 years, Woodlawn United Church has stood—solid and welcoming—in the middle of a Dartmouth, Nova Scotia neighbourhood.

When the church was founded in 1884 it was Methodist. The church was built in a settlement of hardy folks and dusty roads—and in what was beginning to be a booming population built up around shipyards, sawmills and even a factory that produced Canada's first mass-produced ice-skates. That original church, a quaint, white, clapboard building that now boasts a heritage site sign, shares the expansive parking lot with the large, recently renovated brick building. The building was renovated for space and utility, yes, but also to accommodate an aging population for easy coming and going.

These bricks rose into walls in 1959, on the cusp of what would be the heyday of attendance for the United Church of Canada. Remember? Whole families packed into pews. Couples Clubs camping trips. Sunday Schools full to the brim. Flannelgraphs and picnics. Church was just what you did on a Sunday, maybe followed by a slow drive with parents smoking cigarettes in the front seat. Windows rolled up.

Those days are gone. Church is just not what most Canadians habitually do on a Sunday anymore. Phillip and Valerie Kennedy, married in life and teamed in ministry, know this all too well. They have been fighting the good fight of many mainline churches across the country: firing up the defibrillator on a dwindling, aging church population.

It's not like they've given up on Sunday morning. Not at all. This is a fairly healthy United Church after all. But even if the Sabbath is still holy, it's not untouchable. Woodlawn has launched two initiatives to address the time crunch that crashes many a good intention to come to church on a Sunday.

Open Table meets one Saturday night a month. Pizza is involved. "It is an alternative meeting of church," explains Phillip Kennedy. People eat together, then watch a video and follow that with an open discussion. At a recent gathering, they viewed a show about the terrorist attacks on New York City, and then discussed a theology of suffering. They sit around tables of four to six, in a large, light-filled resource room outside of the more formal sanctuary. Kids pile around an arts and crafts table stocked with clay and other tools of the kids-making-a-mess trade.

"It's geared towards people for whom Sunday morning doesn't work. They have hockey practice, lacrosse or a tee time, or whatever," says Kennedy. "Maybe they just want to sleep in because it's their only day to do that. Maybe it's parents with young children who find it hard to get the kids up and going." And for some people, says Kennedy, "regular church worship doesn't do it for them at all."

Then Kennedy asks a question that not every minister would: "Hey, where did 11 o'clock on a Sunday morning come from anyway? The first day of the resurrection for sure, but 11 was after the morning milking. It was not meant to be intrusive on people's working lives."

Society has changed, says Kennedy. "We need to meet people's needs instead of having them meet ours."

Home Church is another way Woodlawn is attempting to meet needs—this time for intimacy, connection and community. Once a month on a Friday night about 20 people (so far), gather at someone's home for a potluck and a discussion. "We're trying to promote the pre-establishment church understanding of faith," says Kennedy. "It is a Way, a building of relationship and deepening of relationship with God and each other. It's more than worship, more than the building. When you share a meal with each other, it takes a relationship to a different level. There's an intimacy in sharing a meal together in a home, that doesn't happen even in a building."

HEY, WHERE DID 11 O'CLOCK ON A SUNDAY MORNING COME FROM ANYWAY?

Aaron Wight is a third-generation Woodlawner. In his early 40s, he is a busy guy, married with two young kids. He has gone with his family to both Open Table and Home Church. He likes them, but Wight is still figuring out where they fit in his family's church attendance.

"Originally, I saw it as an alternative," says Wight. Now, though, after attending both, he and his wife Shannon see the other choices as "in addition to. If we go every Sunday, do we go on a Friday?" he asks. "Do we go to both?" He concedes—like almost every parent everywhere—that Sunday mornings are "a bit of a rush to get the kids up." His kids are busy, Wight says, and "everything in life doesn't work around church schedules anymore." Being able to do something that feeds his family's faith life on the occasional Friday or Saturday night, easing the race to activities like skating, swimming and gymnastics, does have its appeal.

Yet, he's not quite there yet. "The traditional church works for us the most. We know when it is. We know what's involved. We just have to show up. Home Church takes a lot more planning."

Speaking to Wight, you can almost hear the wheels turning as he balances one against the other. "The traditional church, if you're looking for a religious outlet, it's structured. You know what it is, you know what's expected of you." But with Home Church, "It's intimate, it's closer, you have a great dialogue. The minister is right there, you have a really one-on-one atmosphere." Both of them serve their own purpose, Wight concludes. The questions he is left with, the ones Woodlawn is trying to answer, are: "How do you reach out to people? How do you bring them in?"

> "Too many of us are frantically and frenetically running 24/7/365. The costs of this lifestyle are enormous. There is a deeper question though— what is driving our busyness? In other words, what beliefs and values are driving this level of activity? We need to wrestle with and address this question."
>
> – **Steve Brown**,
> President, Arrow Leadership

WOODLAWN UNITED CHURCH
54 Woodlawn Road, Dartmouth, NS | Ph. 902.434.8302
www.woodlawnunited.ca

SHIFTING STATS

MORE TO EXPLORE

 An estimated 87% of Canadian children participate in extracurricular activities.

 More and more Canadians are experiencing what the Canadian Index of Wellbeing at the University of Waterloo calls "a time-crunch." **www.uwaterloo.ca/canadian-index-wellbeing**

 The majority of respondents to a 2013 survey of pastors and members of 16 declining congregations in the US and Canada named competing Sunday activities as "the primary reason for the decline in Sunday worship attendance." 'The Secularization of Sunday: Real or Perceived Competition for Churches.' **www.link.springer.com**

CONCLUSION

The stories in this book are those of missional ministry shining a bright light in Canada—strategic, focused and essential—responding to specific needs and shifting demographics in every corner of our country.

These 40 churches represent 25 denominations in 35 cities, with congregations ranging from 15 to 3500. Some of the churches have been around for a century or more; others are new plants just now burrowing into our challenging Canadian soil.

The *Shifting Stats* big story is that things have changed in Canada. And they have changed in ways we can see and feel, even quantify with numbers and colourful, sobering charts.

We can forgive ourselves in the church world for any moments of panic we may have felt along the way as those things we have taken for granted—our relevance and respect in our communities, even people showing up on a Sunday morning—slip out of our grasp.

But churches, thanks be to God, are responding by doing what churches seem to do best when they are at their very best: meeting needs and loving people.

These churches are, as Michael Frost writes in *The Road to Missional: Journey to the Center of the Church* (Baker Books, 2011), breathing shalom throughout the world, "that we might bring reconciliation and joy, peace and justice to a broken world yearning for redemption."

And that we might bring used couches and casseroles, tips on budgeting and loud music for line dancing, English conversation clubs and rifle lessons, brown bag lunches and crowded potlucks, washing machines and dodge ball games.

This is the Gospel wrapped in service. This is reconciliation and joy in a slow reveal.

"I would have been afraid if I had known what it would grow to be," said Ralph Benson of Evangel Church in Gander, NL. "But I didn't know."

Humility breathes through most of these stories, because the churches truly, actually and often did not know. Asking questions—that great indicator of a humble spirit—was the simple starting point for many of these ministries.

In Charlottetown, PEI, Cornerstone Church noticed the swelling population of immigrants to their lovely city and asked: "How can we help?" Teaming up with the Salvation Army congregation downtown, their next question was: "What can we do together?" Pastor Alfred Reschke in Charlie Lake, BC, asked: "How do we do outreach?" and "Who are we as a church, and how are we going to relate to the community?"

When church planter Ryan Sim set up shop in Ajax, ON, he spent six months in missional listening, that all-senses-alert experience that is, of course, question-based. What needs exist here in this place at this time? What is God doing here already? Where do we fit?

Jamie Arpin-Ricci of Little Flowers Community was asked a question: "When is your church going to have a building?" The answer—from the gut—was that any building this church would have would be an apartment for people living with mental illness.

And that is just what they created.

Questions open up our world. They unlock us. They are behind every great story. Novelists are famous for asking "What if?" as they create plots and people and places that are new and wonderful to this world. But when a church asks "What if?" lives can change forever.

*

The **immigration** stories in this book are all about being responsive. Canada's population is changing. How must the Church change? Robert Young of Bethany Church in Whitehorse, YT said, "If you walk down the road and see different ethnicities, your church should look the same."

Some of the churches in this book host services for their congregants from other countries—providing a haven of word, liturgy and music that reminds our sisters and brothers who have come from so far away of their beloved homes.

Other churches are reaching out to the immigrant populations around them and simply asking, "How can we help?" They are providing practice for English, drives to government offices, clothing, friendship, and in one of the most beautiful ministries we've heard of, asking them what their hopes and dreams are in Altona, MB.

The Hopes and Dreams ministry begins, appropriately enough, where English as a Second Language ends off. Altona Evangelical Mennonite Mission Church is trekking up Maslow's Hierarchy of Needs with their immigrant friends, meeting basic needs but then going to the next level of helping empower goals and dreams.

> **SHIFTING THE IMMIGRATION STATS**
>
> Create Community
> Churches can provide a central gathering place for immigrants, to worship together, but also to share memories, food and speak in their home language.
>
> Minister to the Missing
> Migrant or temporary foreign workers are a hidden population in many communities. They are often desperately lonely for family and friends in their country of origin. The church can be their home away from home.
>
> Find a Partner
> Churches can partner with social service agencies and other groups to meet the needs of new immigrants. This not only provides more effective ways of ministering to migrants, but also positions the church as a vital member of the community.

Churches are helping Canadians wrestle with the time monster by creating alternative worship experiences, like Woodlawn United in Dartmouth, NS, which experiments with Friday and Saturday night events. "Society has changed," said Phillip Kennedy, "We need to meet people's needs instead of having them meet ours." Another United Church congregation, Trinity United in North Bay, ON, acknowledges the time crunch with spontaneous social gatherings announced on Facebook. Those who can, come. And fellowship follows. Churches all across the nation are trying to nurture volunteerism, even while their members have less time available than ever.

The shifting stat of **finances**—almost always involving the crippling experience of debt—is on the minds of many Canadian churches. As it should be. "I think it's naïve of the church to worry about some of the social issues we do without even considering the elephant in the room," said John Cheyne of Faith Tabernacle in Halifax, NS. "There are some issues we are the best equipped as the Christian community to speak on. The Bible has a lot to say about finances, debt, hard work and so on. For many Canadians in our community here, debt or the threat of debt is overwhelming and putting extraordinary strain on families."

The congregations in this book are meeting this particular shifting stat with practical help in the form of those basic essentials of furniture, food and clothing to help Canadians get over a rough patch, but also in creative courses in financial planning and hands-on support in getting to the root of those all too common issues.

It won't surprise you to hear that the very practical financial training ministry offered by North Grenville Community Church in Kemptville, ON, started with two questions after its pastor had attended a financial help course for himself: What if the church offered something like this? And what if it were free?

SHIFTING THE FINANCES / TIME / VOLUNTEERING STATS

Fixing Finances

Churches are recognizing debt and all its burdens as a major issue impacting the lives of Canadians—including in their own congregations. There are many programs available for churches to offer for free in their communities and parishioners are starting to sign up.

Where Did The Time Go?

Churches are recognizing that Canadians have less free time than ever before. Some congregations are experimenting with alternative worship times and hosting events whole families can attend together.

Recognize The Value of Volunteers

Congregations are treating volunteer positions as if they were jobs and valuing this resource highly. Events to honour volunteers, awards of recognition and simply the habit of saying thank you regularly are top priorities for congregations with a healthy volunteer base.

Once again, asking questions led to answers that are changing lives.

When Heidi Billington flew home from a World Vision trip to Haiti where she had viewed youth leading in a way she had never seen in Canada, she asked a what-if that fundamentally changed how Smythe Street Cathedral in Fredericton, NB did its youth ministry. They switched from catering to youth to calling youth to live out their Christian life as if they really believed it.

In all of the **youth** stories in this book, that theme reigned strong.

Remember the moment when Jack Nicholson raged, "You can't handle the truth!" in the movie *A Few Good Men*? More than a few good Canadian churches know that youth can handle much more than we have sometimes offered. At First Baptist Church in Lloydminster, SK, the youth pastor and his team asked themselves what disciples were like and what disciples did. Capture the Flag—however fun it may be— had nothing to do with it. "Games wasn't on our list," said Bute, "so we got rid of them." And at Calvary Church in PEI the thinking goes, if an adult can do it, so can a young person.

Youth are being called to grow through serving, to disciple as they are discipled, and to lead as they are being led.

SHIFTING THE YOUTH STATS

Help Youth Belong

Young adults like to be independent, but they value friendship and, like all of us, a place to belong. Youth who are engaged in the ministries of their church experience a greater sense of belonging.

Provide Purpose

Youth are at a crucial period of searching for purpose in their lives. Empowering youth to be doers of ministry —instead of viewing them as only the recipients—engages them more deeply in their faith.

> ### Flexibility is Key
> Youth culture is in a state of constant transition. Churches that are willing to adapt and take risks—often at the expense of losing those who prefer the comfort of "the way it's always been done"—will succeed in remaining relevant to young people.

If youth are being challenged, than **families** are being cared for. This is what we saw in our research. Churches are recognizing that families need attention, perhaps like never before. The ministries we heard of ranged from caring for single parents—Middleton, NS has a wonderful, loving ministry built from a template they tweaked for their own needs—to teaching married couples how to have a healthy sex life and a good fight, like at New Joy Church in Vancouver, BC.

> ### SHIFTING THE FAMILY STATS
>
> #### Families Have Changed – So Should Family Ministry
> Family ministry today looks different than it ever has. Churches are paying attention to divorced, single-parent and never-married family configurations.
>
> #### There's No Need to Reinvent the Wheel
> Churches are running ministries that come "pre-packaged" but tweaking the program to fit their own culture and needs.
>
> #### Maximize Family Time
> With the busy schedule of many Canadian families, churches are looking for alternative time slots for worship experiences, and also providing social times for the whole family, not just youth or couples.

Perhaps not surprisingly, the most difficult churches to locate for this project were the ones doing innovative ministry in the shifting stats of **technology**. Churches don't tend to be famous for being ahead of the technology curve. But that is exactly what Église Nouvelle Vie is trying to be as they curate a website that is a ministry unto itself, beautiful and sleek with resources to help those in all kinds of need. It is technology as ministry. Their Facebook feed is just as active and rich.

Redeem the Commute out of Ajax, ON, harnesses technology to meet people right where they are at, staring into their mobile devices as they take the GO Train to Toronto. And Kensington Commons in Calgary, AB, invited the city to charge their devices when the power went out, recognizing that Canadians practically lead the world in living online.

What a practical, simple and responsive idea. Those three words describe the majority of the stories in this book.

SHIFTING THE TECHNOLOGY STATS

Taking On The Tech Challenge

Technology is a gift, a mystery and a challenge still to many churches. Harnessing its power well for Canadian congregations is an ongoing challenge. Don't be afraid to dip your toes in the technology pool and learn as you go.

Begin With The Web

Websites are often the first stop for Canadians searching for churches and all they have to offer. Keeping the site simple and inviting with up to date information needs to be a priority for churches on the web.

Going Social

Some churches view social media as a front door to a whole new population: the online community. The key to remaining effective on social media is responsiveness. Be prepared to not only post information, but to engage with those who are following you online.

As journalists who are Christian, our work routinely involves asking questions of churches and their leaders. We research churches and what they are facing and doing in Canada today. We've been doing it for years.

The stories are not always good. How could they possibly be? These stories, though, are some of the best we have heard in a while. As we wrap up this project, we wanted to share with readers some of the key lessons we are taking away from this experience. This is what we heard again and again.

- The size of your church truly does not matter. Small churches are doing very big things. We really like that.

- Partnerships are often there for the making—even with government agencies. When churches, in humility, approached other organizations and asked how they could help, they were generally invited on board.

- Don't believe that the Church does not matter. It matters greatly in communities across Canada. There are many people whose lives are being significantly helped because a humble church asked simple questions.

- Listen, then do. We learned that the Church is heard best when it listens first.

We love the Church. Yes, the Church is but a dim reflection and yes, we are a sorry, motley crew. In all the Church's glorious imperfections, we do see God's glory still. And it is shining brightly in Canada.

POSTSCRIPT

REV. DR. DON MOORE
National Church Ambassador,
World Vision Canada

How exciting to learn from these stories how 40 churches are adapting to the changing realities in our Canadian landscape. If you find yourself feeling inspired by any of these stories, let me encourage you in your desire to create something new in your church for the sake of your community.

God has provided us with an excellent example in how to bring about lasting change through the life and leadership of Nehemiah.

Looking at the early chapters of the book of Nehemiah, one can readily identify a seven-step change process that God used to accomplish His purposes for change. Remember the backstory: God's people had been exiled to Babylon leaving their city of Jerusalem far behind where life and conditions had deteriorated.

A significant need for change is identified and a seven-step change process begins. Here's where Nehemiah's story begins.

Awareness of a Significant Need for Change
(Nehemiah 1:1-4)

Nehemiah's brother has just returned from a trip to Judah when he delivers that heartbreaking news that Jerusalem, the city of their God, is in desperate condition and is literally falling apart. Notice that this need for change comes with solid source credibility (1:2) a clear description of the need (1:3) and results in an inner emotional response that soon becomes apparent to all (1:4).

Acknowledgement of his own inadequacy
(Nehemiah 1:4-11)

Nehemiah immediately recognizes his own inadequacy and need for God's help. He begins with worship of the Almighty (1:5), confession of his failures and those of his people (1:6-7), a claim of God's promises (1:8-9) and a specific request for help in bringing about changes (1:10-11). I believe it is during this time that God gives him insight into what is to follow.

Approval from the Key Influencers/Stakeholders
(Nehemiah 2:1-10)

Using the influence he has developed over the years, Nehemiah begins by seeking the most influential support to which he has access (2:1-3), even at great risk to his own life. Just as he is to make his pitch to the king, under his breath he prays (2:4), making his request clear and specific (2:5-8). In return, he receives approval and the assistance needed to begin to bring change to Jerusalem (2:7-9). Resistance to change is already emerging (2:10).

Analysis of the Situation
(Nehemiah 2:11-16)

Arriving in Jerusalem, Nehemiah recognizes the importance of possessing a clear understanding of this situation. Under cover of night, with a few friends, he conducts an inspection (2:11-12), resulting in a careful analysis of what will be required to bring about the significant change that will be needed (2:13-

16). More than likely it was at this point when Nehemiah and his trusted leaders developed a specific plan of action.

Announcement of the Need for Change
(Nehemiah 2:17-18)

As Nehemiah shares publicly what he has learned from spending time in God's presence, it's no surprise that the people immediately recognize God's inspired action plan (2:17). Their full support for this vision for change is clear in both word and their willingness to act immediately (2:18).

Antagonism towards God's people and their action
(Nehemiah 2:19-20)

As soon as the plan for change is announced, opposition emerges (as it often does when God is at work in His people). Empowered by God and His people, Nehemiah responds with a voice of authority and a clear statement of intention, putting the opposition in their place (2:20).

Accomplishment of the Significant Change
(Nehemiah 6:15-16)

The mission is accomplished (6:15) in only 52 days, even though the opposition persists (6:16).

I've used this Biblical process for change both in my personal life and also in the churches and ministries I've been privileged to lead over the years. Each time as I become aware of a need for change, I go to our Heavenly Father for His perspective. For a God who never changes, I've discovered He is full of surprises in the way in which He leads me to guide the change process.

STORY MATRIX

BY STORY THEME
BY REGION
BY DENOMINATION
BY CHURCH SIZE

⇨ BY STORY THEME

FAMILY

UNLEASHING THE POTENTIAL OF KIDS IN FREDERICTON
Smythe Street Cathedral | Fredericton, NB
Chapter 2 15

STRENGTHENING FAITH AND ABORIGINAL CULTURE
St. Jude's Anglican Cathedral | Iqaluit, NU
Chapter 6 41

RENOVATED ROOMS – AND RESTORED LIVES
Little Flowers Community | Winnipeg, MB
Chapter 10 65

STRONG MARRIAGES, STRONG COMMUNITY
New Joy Church | Richmond, BC
Chapter 15 97

EMPOWERING KIDS AND STRENGTHENING FAMILIES
Calvary Church | Charlottetown, PE
Chapter 21 133

FLOURISHING FAMILIES AND FRIENDSHIPS
Trinity United Church | North Bay, ON
Chapter 27 171

MINISTRY IN AN UNEXPECTED PLACE
Grandview Calvary Baptist | Vancouver, BC
Chapter 32 201

SINGLE PARENTS: BUILDING BRIDGES
Emmanuel Congregational Christian Church | Middleton, NS
Chapter 36 225

ADOPTIVE AND FOSTER FAMILIES FINDING HOPE
First Alliance Church | Calgary, AB
Chapter 39 243

💲 FINANCES

COACHING AND CONNECTING TO TACKLE DEBT
North Grenville Community Church | Kemptville, ON
Chapter 13 85

FURNISHING WITH LOVE IN GANDER
Evangel Church | Gander, NL
Chapter 23 147

SHOTS AND SWAPS
Charlie Lake Community Church | Charlie Lake, BC
Chapter 28 177

DROWNING IN DEBT – LIFTED BY FAITH
Faith Tabernacle | Halifax, NS
Chapter 31 195

BENEVOLENCE WITHOUT BRANDING
Hillcrest Evangelical Missionary Church | Medicine Hat, AB
Chapter 34 213

✈ IMMIGRATION

OPENING DOORS TO NEW IMMIGRANTS
Gateway Church | Mississauga, ON
Chapter 3 21

REFUGEE RELIEF IN SASKATOON
Meadowgreen House for All Nations | Saskatoon, SK
Chapter 7 47

IMMIGRANTS: WELCOME TO THE ISLAND
Cornerstone Baptist Church | Charlottetown, PE
Chapter 12 77

MAKING ROOM IN CANADA'S NORTH
Bethany Church | Whitehorse, YT
Chapter 18 115

ALL IN THE FAMILY
Eglise Chretienne du Plateau | Gatineau, QC
Chapter 22 139

JESUS ISN'T ONLY FOR WHITE PEOPLE
The Life Centre | Abbotsford, BC
Chapter 26 165

BECOMING "MIGHTY NEIGHBOURLY"
Lake Ridge Community | Chestermere, AB
Chapter 30 189

WELCOMING DIVERSITY IN WINNIPEG
Immanuel Lutheran Church | Winnipeg, MB
Chapter 35 219

HARVESTING FRUIT AND FRIENDSHIP
Southridge Community Church | St. Catharines, ON
Chapter 38 237

🖥 TECHNOLOGY

REACHING THE WEB, REACHING THE WORLD
Eglise Nouvelle Vie | Longueil, QC
Chapter 5 35

A PODCAST CAN CHANGE YOUR WORLD
Rock Church | Lower Sackville, NS
Chapter 11 71

TEXTING FOR TRUTH
Kensington Commons Church | Calgary, AB
Chapter 17 109

MAKING DIGITAL CONNECTIONS
Grant Memorial Church | Winnipeg, MB
Chapter 25 159

SMALL CHURCH – BIG TECH IMPACT
Redeemer Church | Ajax, ON
Chapter 33 207

⏲ TIME / VOLUNTEERING

TOUCHING LIVES BY TAPPING SHOULDERS
Altona Evangelical Mennonite Mission Church | Altona, MB
Chapter 4 27

ENGAGING HANDS AND HEARTS IN COMMUNITY
Wolf Creek Community Church | Lacombe, AB
Chapter 9 59

WATCHING VOLUNTEERS FLY IN MONCTON
Moncton Wesleyan Church | Moncton, NB
Chapter 16 103

PURGE SUNDAYS: INNIES AND OUTIES
The Meeting House | Oakville, ON
Chapter 20 127

CRASHING THE TIME CRUNCH
Woodlawn United Church | Dartmouth, NS
Chapter 40 249

🧍 YOUTH

NOURISHING STUDENT BODIES – AND SOULS
Emmanuel Baptist Church | Victoria, BC
Chapter 1 9

CULTIVATING COMPASSION – CREATING KOINONIA
St. Paul's Presbyterian Church | Ottawa, ON
Chapter 8 53

ENGAGING YOUTH – BUILDING RELATIONSHIPS
Compass Church | Regina, SK
Chapter 14 91

RESHAPING TRADITION – REVITALIZING YOUTH
Saint Benedict Parish | Halifax, NS
Chapter 19 121

IT'S MORE THAN JUST A MEAL
Parish of the Nerepis & St. John, Church of the Resurrection
St. Paul's and St. Peter's | Grand Bay, NB
Chapter 24 153

CAMPING IN PARADISE
Dene Pentecostal Church | Hay River, NT
Chapter 29 183

HOW "CHRISTIAN" BECAME MORE THAN JUST A NAME
First Baptist Church Lloydminster | Lloydminster, SK
Chapter 37 231

⇨ BY REGION

NEWFOUNDLAND & LABRADOR

FURNISHING WITH LOVE IN GANDER
Evangel Church | Gander, NL
Chapter 23 147

NOVA SCOTIA

A PODCAST CAN CHANGE YOUR WORLD
Rock Church | Lower Sackville, NS
Chapter 11 71

RESHAPING TRADITION – REVITALIZING YOUTH
Saint Benedict Parish | Halifax, NS
Chapter 19 121

DROWNING IN DEBT – LIFTED BY FAITH
Faith Tabernacle | Halifax, NS
Chapter 31 195

SINGLE PARENTS: BUILDING BRIDGES
Emmanuel Congregational Christian Church | Middleton, NS
Chapter 36 225

CRASHING THE TIME CRUNCH
Woodlawn United Church | Dartmouth, NS
Chapter 40 249

NEW BRUNSWICK

UNLEASHING THE POTENTIAL OF KIDS IN FREDERICTON
Smythe Street Cathedral | Fredericton, NB
Chapter 2 15

WATCHING VOLUNTEERS FLY IN MONCTON
Moncton Wesleyan Church | Moncton, NB
Chapter 16 103

IT'S MORE THAN JUST A MEAL
Parish of the Nerepis & St. John, Church of the Resurrection St. Paul's and St. Peter's | Grand Bay, NB
Chapter 24 153

PRINCE EDWARD ISLAND

IMMIGRANTS: WELCOME TO THE ISLAND
Cornerstone Baptist Church | Charlottetown, PE
Chapter 12 77

EMPOWERING KIDS AND STRENGTHENING FAMILIES
Calvary Church | Charlottetown, PE
Chapter 21 133

QUEBEC

REACHING THE WEB, REACHING THE WORLD
Eglise Nouvelle Vie | Longueil, QC
Chapter 5 35

ALL IN THE FAMILY
Eglise Chretienne du Plateau | Gatineau, QC
Chapter 22 139

ONTARIO

OPENING DOORS TO NEW IMMIGRANTS
Gateway Church | Mississauga, ON
Chapter 3 21

CULTIVATING COMPASSION – CREATING KOINONIA
St. Paul's Presbyterian Church | Ottawa, ON
Chapter 8 53

COACHING AND CONNECTING TO TACKLE DEBT
North Grenville Community Church | Kemptville, ON
Chapter 13 85

PURGE SUNDAYS: INNIES AND OUTIES
The Meeting House | Oakville, ON
Chapter 20 127

FLOURISHING FAMILIES AND FRIENDSHIPS
Trinity United Church | North Bay, ON
Chapter 27 171

SMALL CHURCH – BIG TECH IMPACT
Redeemer Church | Ajax, ON
Chapter 33 207

HARVESTING FRUIT AND FRIENDSHIP
Southridge Community Church | St. Catharines, ON
Chapter 38 237

MANITOBA

TOUCHING LIVES BY TAPPING SHOULDERS
Altona Evangelical Mennonite Mission Church | Altona, MB
Chapter 4 27

RENOVATED ROOMS – AND RESTORED LIVES
Little Flowers Community | Winnipeg, MB
Chapter 10 65

MAKING DIGITAL CONNECTIONS
Grant Memorial Church | Winnipeg, MB
Chapter 25 159

WELCOMING DIVERSITY IN WINNIPEG
Immanuel Lutheran Church | Winnipeg, MB
Chapter 35 219

SASKATCHEWAN

REFUGEE RELIEF IN SASKATOON
Meadowgreen House for All Nations | Saskatoon, SK
Chapter 7 47

ENGAGING YOUTH – BUILDING RELATIONSHIPS
Compass Church | Regina, SK
Chapter 14 91

HOW "CHRISTIAN" BECAME MORE THAN JUST A NAME
First Baptist Church Lloydminster | Lloydminster, SK
Chapter 37 231

ALBERTA

ENGAGING HANDS AND HEARTS IN COMMUNITY
Wolf Creek Community Church | Lacombe, AB
Chapter 9 59

TEXTING FOR TRUTH
Kensington Commons Church | Calgary, AB
Chapter 17 109

BECOMING "MIGHTY NEIGHBOURLY"
Lake Ridge Community | Chestermere, AB
Chapter 30 189

BENEVOLENCE WITHOUT BRANDING
Hillcrest Evangelical Missionary Church | Medicine Hat, AB
Chapter 34 213

ADOPTIVE AND FOSTER FAMILIES FINDING HOPE
First Alliance Church | Calgary, AB
Chapter 39 243

BRITISH COLUMBIA

NOURISHING STUDENT BODIES – AND SOULS
Emmanuel Baptist Church | Victoria, BC
Chapter 1 9

STRONG MARRIAGES, STRONG COMMUNITY
New Joy Church | Richmond, BC
Chapter 15 97

JESUS ISN'T ONLY FOR WHITE PEOPLE
The Life Centre | Abbotsford, BC
Chapter 26 165

SHOTS AND SWAPS
Charlie Lake Community Church | Charlie Lake, BC
Chapter 28 177

MINISTRY IN AN UNEXPECTED PLACE
Grandview Calvary Baptist | Vancouver, BC
Chapter 32 201

NORTHWEST TERRITORIES

CAMPING IN PARADISE
Dene Pentecostal Church | Hay River, NT
Chapter 29 183

NUNUVUT

STRENGTHENING FAITH AND ABORIGINAL CULTURE
St. Jude's Anglican Cathedral | Iqaluit, NU
Chapter 6 41

YUKON

MAKING ROOM IN CANADA'S NORTH
Bethany Church | Whitehorse, YT
Chapter 18 115

⇨ BY DENOMINATION

ANGLICAN CHURCH OF CANADA

STRENGTHENING FAITH AND ABORIGINAL CULTURE
St. Jude's Anglican Cathedral | Iqaluit, NU
Chapter 6 41

IT'S MORE THAN JUST A MEAL
Parish of the Nerepis & St. John, Church of the Resurrection St. Paul's and St. Peter's | Grand Bay, NB
Chapter 24 153

SMALL CHURCH – BIG TECH IMPACT
Redeemer Church | Ajax, ON
Chapter 33 207

ASSOCIATION CHRÉTIENNE POUR LA FRANCOPHONIE

REACHING THE WEB, REACHING THE WORLD
Église Nouvelle Vie | Longueil, QC
Chapter 5 35

BAPTIST GENERAL CONFERENCE OF CANADA

REFUGEE RELIEF IN SASKATOON
Meadowgreen House for All Nations | Saskatoon, SK
Chapter 7 47

MAKING DIGITAL CONNECTIONS
Grant Memorial Church | Winnipeg, MB
Chapter 25 159

BRETHREN IN CHRIST

PURGE SUNDAYS: INNIES AND OUTIES
The Meeting House | Oakville, ON
Chapter 20 127

CANADIAN BAPTIST MINISTRIES

MINISTRY IN AN UNEXPECTED PLACE
Grandview Calvary Baptist | Vancouver, BC
Chapter 32 201

CANADIAN BAPTISTS OF WESTERN CANADA

NOURISHING STUDENT BODIES – AND SOULS
Emmanuel Baptist Church | Victoria, BC
Chapter 1 9

SHOTS AND SWAPS
Charlie Lake Community Church | Charlie Lake, BC
Chapter 28 177

CANADIAN CONFERENCE OF MENNONITE BRETHREN CHURCHES

JESUS ISN'T ONLY FOR WHITE PEOPLE
The Life Centre | Abbotsford, BC
Chapter 26 165

HARVESTING FRUIT AND FRIENDSHIP
Southridge Community Church | St. Catharines, ON
Chapter 38 237

CHRISTIAN & MISSIONARY ALLIANCE IN CANADA

ADOPTIVE AND FOSTER FAMILIES FINDING HOPE
First Alliance Church | Calgary, AB
Chapter 39 243

CHRISTIAN REFORMED CHURCH

ENGAGING HANDS AND HEARTS IN COMMUNITY
Wolf Creek Community Church | Lacombe, AB
Chapter 9 59

CHURCH PLANTING MINISTRIES INC.

OPENING DOORS TO NEW IMMIGRANTS
Gateway Church | Mississauga, ON
Chapter 3 21

CONGREGATIONAL CHRISTIAN CHURCHES OF CANADA

SINGLE PARENTS: BUILDING BRIDGES
Emmanuel Congregational Christian Church | Middleton, NS
Chapter 36 225

CONVENTION OF ATLANTIC BAPTIST CHURCHES

IMMIGRANTS: WELCOME TO THE ISLAND
Cornerstone Baptist Church | Charlottetown, PE
Chapter 12 77

EVANGELICAL COVENANT CHURCHES OF CANADA

TEXTING FOR TRUTH
Kensington Commons Church | Calgary, AB
Chapter 17 109

BECOMING "MIGHTY NEIGHBOURLY"
Lake Ridge Community | Chestermere, AB
Chapter 30 189

EVANGELICAL MENNONITE MISSION CONFERENCE

TOUCHING LIVES BY TAPPING SHOULDERS
Altona Evangelical Mennonite Mission Church | Altona, MB
Chapter 4 27

EVANGELICAL MISSIONARY CHURCH

BENEVOLENCE WITHOUT BRANDING
Hillcrest Evangelical Missionary Church | Medicine Hat, AB
Chapter 34 213

FELLOWSHIP OF EVANGELICAL BAPTIST CHURCHES OF CANADA

HOW "CHRISTIAN" BECAME MORE THAN JUST A NAME
First Baptist Church Lloydminster | Lloydminster, SK
Chapter 37 231

FREE METHODIST CHURCH IN CANADA

COACHING AND CONNECTING TO TACKLE DEBT
North Grenville Community Church | Kemptville, ON
Chapter 13 85

LUTHERAN CHURCH CANADA

WELCOMING DIVERSITY IN WINNIPEG
Immanuel Lutheran Church | Winnipeg, MB
Chapter 35 219

MENNONITE CHURCH CANADA

RENOVATED ROOMS – AND RESTORED LIVES
Little Flowers Community | Winnipeg, MB
Chapter 10 65

NON-DENOMINATIONAL

UNLEASHING THE POTENTIAL OF KIDS IN FREDERICTON
Smythe Street Cathedral | Fredericton, NB
Chapter 2 15

A PODCAST CAN CHANGE YOUR WORLD
Rock Church | Lower Sackville, NS
Chapter 11 71

ENGAGING YOUTH – BUILDING RELATIONSHIPS
Compass Church | Regina, SK
Chapter 14 91

STRONG MARRIAGES, STRONG COMMUNITY
New Joy Church | Richmond, BC
Chapter 15 97

PENTECOSTAL ASSEMBLIES OF CANADA

MAKING ROOM IN CANADA'S NORTH
Bethany Church | Whitehorse, YT
Chapter 18 115

EMPOWERING KIDS AND STRENGTHENING FAMILIES
Calvary Church | Charlottetown, PE
Chapter 21 133

CAMPING IN PARADISE
Dene Pentecostal Church | Hay River, NT
Chapter 29 183

DROWNING IN DEBT – LIFTED BY FAITH
Faith Tabernacle | Halifax, NS
Chapter 31 195

PENTECOSTAL ASSEMBLIES OF NEWFOUNDLAND

FURNISHING WITH LOVE IN GANDER
Evangel Church | Gander, NL
Chapter 23 147

PRESBYTERIAN CHURCH IN CANADA

CULTIVATING COMPASSION – CREATING KOINONIA
St. Paul's Presbyterian Church | Ottawa, ON
Chapter 8 53

ROMAN CATHOLIC CHURCH

RESHAPING TRADITION – REVITALIZING YOUTH
Saint Benedict Parish | Halifax, NS
Chapter 19 121

UNION OF FRENCH BAPTIST CHURCHES OF CANADA

ALL IN THE FAMILY
Eglise Chretienne du Plateau | Gatineau, QC
Chapter 22 139

UNITED CHURCH OF CANADA

FLOURISHING FAMILIES AND FRIENDSHIPS
Trinity United Church | North Bay, ON
Chapter 27 171

CRASHING THE TIME CRUNCH
Woodlawn United Church | Dartmouth, NS
Chapter 40 249

THE WESLEYAN CHURCH

WATCHING VOLUNTEERS FLY IN MONCTON
Moncton Wesleyan Church | Moncton, NB
Chapter 16 103

⇨ BY CHURCH SIZE

1-199

NOURISHING STUDENT BODIES – AND SOULS
Emmanuel Baptist Church | Victoria, BC
Chapter 1 9

OPENING DOORS TO NEW IMMIGRANTS
Gateway Church | Mississauga, ON
Chapter 3 21

REFUGEE RELIEF IN SASKATOON
Meadowgreen House for All Nations | Saskatoon, SK
Chapter 7 47

ENGAGING HANDS AND HEARTS IN COMMUNITY
Wolf Creek Community Church | Lacombe, AB
Chapter 9 59

RENOVATED ROOMS – AND RESTORED LIVES
Little Flowers Community | Winnipeg, MB
Chapter 10 65

COACHING AND CONNECTING TO TACKLE DEBT
North Grenville Community Church | Kemptville, ON
Chapter 13 85

ENGAGING YOUTH – BUILDING RELATIONSHIPS
Compass Church | Regina, SK
Chapter 14 91

EMPOWERING KIDS AND STRENGTHENING FAMILIES
Calvary Church | Charlottetown, PE
Chapter 21 133

IT'S MORE THAN JUST A MEAL
Parish of the Nerepis & St. John, Church of the Resurrection St. Paul's and St. Peter's | Grand Bay, NB
Chapter 24 153

JESUS ISN'T ONLY FOR WHITE PEOPLE
The Life Centre | Abbotsford, BC
Chapter 26 165

SHOTS AND SWAPS
Charlie Lake Community Church | Charlie Lake, BC
Chapter 28 177

CAMPING IN PARADISE
Dene Pentecostal Church | Hay River, NT
Chapter 29 183

BECOMING "MIGHTY NEIGHBOURLY"
Lake Ridge Community | Chestermere, AB
Chapter 30 189

MINISTRY IN AN UNEXPECTED PLACE
Grandview Calvary Baptist | Vancouver, BC
Chapter 32 201

SMALL CHURCH – BIG TECH IMPACT
Redeemer Church | Ajax, ON
Chapter 33 207

WELCOMING DIVERSITY IN WINNIPEG
Immanuel Lutheran Church | Winnipeg, MB
Chapter 35 219

SINGLE PARENTS: BUILDING BRIDGES
Emmanuel Congregational Christian Church | Middleton, NS
Chapter 36 225

200-499

STRENGTHENING FAITH AND ABORIGINAL CULTURE
St. Jude's Anglican Cathedral | Iqaluit, NU
Chapter 6 41

CULTIVATING COMPASSION – CREATING KOINONIA
St. Paul's Presbyterian Church | Ottawa, ON
Chapter 8 53

IMMIGRANTS: WELCOME TO THE ISLAND
Cornerstone Baptist Church | Charlottetown, PE
Chapter 12 77

STRONG MARRIAGES, STRONG COMMUNITY
New Joy Church | Richmond, BC
Chapter 15 97

TEXTING FOR TRUTH
Kensington Commons Church | Calgary, AB
Chapter 17 109

MAKING ROOM IN CANADA'S NORTH
Bethany Church | Whitehorse, YT
Chapter 18 115

ALL IN THE FAMILY
Eglise Chretienne du Plateau | Gatineau, QC
Chapter 22 139

FURNISHING WITH LOVE IN GANDER
Evangel Church | Gander, NL
Chapter 23 147

FLOURISHING FAMILIES AND FRIENDSHIPS
Trinity United Church | North Bay, ON
Chapter 27 171

DROWNING IN DEBT – LIFTED BY FAITH
Faith Tabernacle | Halifax, NS
Chapter 31 195

HOW "CHRISTIAN" BECAME MORE THAN JUST A NAME
First Baptist Church Lloydminster | Lloydminster, SK
Chapter 37 231

HARVESTING FRUIT AND FRIENDSHIP
Southridge Community Church | St. Catharines, ON
Chapter 38 237

CRASHING THE TIME CRUNCH
Woodlawn United Church | Dartmouth, NS
Chapter 40 249

500-999

UNLEASHING THE POTENTIAL OF KIDS IN FREDERICTON
Smythe Street Cathedral | Fredericton, NB
Chapter 2 15

TOUCHING LIVES BY TAPPING SHOULDERS
Altona Evangelical Mennonite Mission Church | Altona, MB
Chapter 4 27

A PODCAST CAN CHANGE YOUR WORLD
Rock Church | Lower Sackville, NS
Chapter 11 71

BENEVOLENCE WITHOUT BRANDING
Hillcrest Evangelical Missionary Church | Medicine Hat, AB
Chapter 34 213

1000-1999

WATCHING VOLUNTEERS FLY IN MONCTON
Moncton Wesleyan Church | Moncton, NB
Chapter 16 103

RESHAPING TRADITION – REVITALIZING YOUTH
Saint Benedict Parish | Halifax, NS
Chapter 19 121

MAKING DIGITAL CONNECTIONS
Grant Memorial Church | Winnipeg, MB
Chapter 25 159

2000+

REACHING THE WEB, REACHING THE WORLD
Eglise Nouvelle Vie | Longueil, QC
Chapter 5 35

PURGE SUNDAYS: INNIES AND OUTIES
The Meeting House | Oakville, ON
Chapter 20 127

ADOPTIVE AND FOSTER FAMILIES FINDING HOPE
First Alliance Church | Calgary, AB
Chapter 39 243

AUTHORS

Patricia Paddey is a freelance writer, editor and communications consultant. With a background in broadcast journalism, she has worked her entire career with mainstream and niche media. Currently, she is a partner in the Canadian Christian News Service, a senior writer at *Faith Today* magazine and serves part-time as communications director for Save the Mothers. She is pursuing a Master of Theological Studies part-time at McMaster Divinity College. Paddey lives with her husband Doug in Mississauga, ON. They have three young adult children.

Karen Stiller is a freelance writer and editor, and a senior editor of *Faith Today* magazine. She is author of *Going Missional: Conversations with 13 Canadian Churches who Have Embraced Missional Life* and managing editor of *Evangelicals Around the World: A Global Handbook for the 21st Century* (Thomas Nelson, 2015).

Stiller is also a partner in the Canadian Christian News Service and communications manager for Langham Partnership Canada. She was the recipient of the 2012 A.C. Forrest Memorial Award for excellence in religious journalism. Stiller lives in Port Perry, ON, with her husband Brent and their children.

Rev Dr Don Moore serves as the National Church Ambassador with World Vision Canada. Formerly he served as Professor of Education and the founding Dean of the Seminary at Briercrest Family of Schools in Saskatchewan.

Previously Don served as the Vice President for Leadership Development and Care with The Navigators of Canada. In addition, he led a national movement of more than 120 national faith leaders in Vision 2000 Canada under the auspices of the Evangelical Fellowship of Canada.

Don's passion is to inspire vision and explore partnership opportunities with denominational and senior church leaders. His aspiration is to assist churches in accomplishing their missional goals, both in Canada and around the world.

EQUIPPING LEADERS TO LEAD

Churches are the primary instrument for God's work in the world. Because we affirm this truth at World Vision, our team wants to help equip you as a leader for mission. Visit our website to discover a variety of ways to stay connected, including:

ANNUAL CHURCH LEADERS FORUM

Our flagship leadership event reaches hundreds of leaders across Canada each spring. For more than seven years, the Annual Church Leaders Forums have been a great opportunity to connect with peers and learn from ministry specialists.

RESPONDING CHURCH LEADERS NETWORK

As a ministry leader stay on top of what's happening both locally and globally when it comes to meeting the needs of those living with poverty and injustice. Receive monthly email updates to encourage and inspire you in your leadership role. Features include engaging blogs, free resources and advance notice of special events.

REGIONAL CHURCH ADVISORS

Your regional church advisor is interested in learning about and supporting your church's missional goals. Our team of church advisors has a wide range of resources on which to draw and is equipped to assist you in your ministry. There's a church advisor in your area available to serve you.

MINISTRY RESOURCES

From personal devotional books to small group studies, we offer a range of resources to unlock your church's heart of love. Resources such as *Choose Justice*, a six-session DVD study featuring Tony Campolo and Shane Claiborne and *Jesus on Justice* by Dr. Don Posterski, will equip you and your congregation to respond to the needs of our broken world.

To learn more, visit www.churches.worldvision.ca **or email us at** churchengagement@worldvision.ca**.**